Developing Core Literacy Proficiencies

GRADE 7

Student Edition

GRADE 7

STUDENT EDITION

Developing Core Literacy Proficiencies

ODELL EDUCATION

JOSSEY-BASS™
A Wiley Brand

Published by Jossey-Bass

A Wiley Brand

One Montgomery Street, Suite 1000, San Francisco, CA 94104-4594—www.josseybass.com

Jossey-Bass books and products are available through most bookstores. To contact Jossey-Bass directly call our Customer Care Department within the U.S. at 800-956-7739, outside the U.S. at 317-572-3986, or fax 317-572-4002.

Wiley publishes in a variety of print and electronic formats and by print-on-demand. Some material included with standard print versions of this book may not be included in e-books or in print-on-demand. If this book refers to media such as a CD or DVD that is not included in the version you purchased, you may download this material at www.wiley.com/go/coreliteracy (use the following password: odell2016). For more information about Wiley products, visit www.wiley.com.

Library of Congress Cataloging-in-Publication Data

Names: Odell Education, author.
Title: Developing core literacy proficiencies. Grade 7 / Odell Education.
Description: Student edition. | San Francisco, CA : Jossey-Bass, 2016.
Identifiers: LCCN 2016002098 (print) | LCCN 2016012513 (ebook) |
  ISBN 9781119192565 (paperback) | ISBN 9781119192596 (pdf) | ISBN 9781119192572 (epub)
Subjects: LCSH: Language arts (Middle school)—Curricula—United States. |
  Common Core State Standards (Education)
Classification: LCC LB1631 .O37 2016 (print) | LCC LB1631 (ebook) | DDC
  428.0071/2—dc23
LC record available at http://lccn.loc.gov/2016002098

Cover Design: Wiley
Cover Image: ©Danae Olaso/EyeEm/Getty Images, Inc.

Printed in the United States of America

FIRST EDITION

PB Printing   10 9 8 7 6 5 4 3 2 1

ACKNOWLEDGMENTS

Project director: Stephanie Smythe

Primary program designers:

- Rick Dills, EdD
- Judson Odell
- Ioana Radoi
- Daniel Fennessy

Curriculum consultant: Nemeesha Brown

Unit developers—Texts, notes, and questions:

- Reading Closely for Textual Details, "We reckoned now that we were at the Pole" Rick Dills, EdD
- Making Evidence-Based Claims, "We organized!": Rick Dills, EdD
- Researching to Deepen Understanding, Water: Why is it so valuable?: Luke Bauer
- Building Evidence-Based Arguments, "Doping can be that last 2 percent": Luke Bauer

We are grateful for feedback we received on early versions of units from Achieve's EQuIP Review Process, under the direction of Christine Tell, Alissa Peltzman, and Cristina Marks.

We are also grateful for the students and teachers of the Bay Shore Schools who collaborated with us to pilot the curriculum. Thanks especially to LaQuita Outlaw, Elizabeth Galarza, Caitlin Moreira, and Jen Ritter (who personally renamed the **Supporting Evidence-Based Claims Tool**).

We are especially grateful for New York State and the Regents Research Fund for funding the development of the earlier Open Educational Resource version of this curriculum. Without the support we received from Kristen Huff, David Abel, and Kate Gerson, none of this work would have been possible.

CONTENTS

Acknowledgments   v

Introduction to the Core Literacy Proficiencies: Becoming a Literate Person   viii

Unit 1:   Reading Closely for Textual Details: "We reckoned now that we were at the Pole"   **1**
    Goal   2
    Topic   2
    Activities   2
Reading Closely for Textual Details Unit Texts   5
    Text 1: Robert Falcon Scott and Roald Amundsen Images   7
    Text 2: *The Last Expedition*, Ch. V, Robert Falcon Scott   9
    Text 3: *Roald Amundsen South Pole,* Viking River Cruises   11
    Text 4: *Scott's Hut and the Explorer's Heritage of Antarctica*, UNESCO
    World Wonders Project   11
    Text 5: *The North Pole*, Ch. XXI, Robert Peary   12
    Text 6: *"To Build a Fire"*, Jack London   15
    Text 7: *The South Pole*, Ch. XII, Roald Amundsen   19
    Text 8: *Scott's Last Expedition*, Ch. XVIII, Robert Falcon Scott   22
    Text 9: *Scott's Last Expedition,* Ch. XX, Robert Falcon Scott   25
Reading Closely Literacy Toolbox   36

Unit 2:   Making Evidence-Based Claims: "We organized!"   **77**
    Goal   78
    Topic   78
    Activities   78
Making Evidence-Based Claims Unit Texts   81
    Excerpt of "I've Been to the Mountaintop" speech, Dr. Martin Luther King Jr.   81
    Excerpt of 1984 Commonwealth Club Address, Cesar Chavez   91
    Excerpt of "A Single Garment of Destiny" address, Janet Murguia   99
Making Evidence-Based Claims Literacy Toolbox   108

Unit 3:   Researching to Deepen Understanding: Water: Why is it so valuable?   **151**
    Goal   152
    Topic   152
    Activities   152
Researching to Deepen Understanding Common Source Set   156
Researching to Deepen Understanding Literacy Toolbox   162

Unit 4:   Building Evidence-Based Arguments: "Doping can be that last 2 percent"   **229**
    Goal   230
    Topic   230
    Activities   230
Building Evidence-Based Arguments Unit Texts   233
Building Evidence-Based Arguments Literacy Toolbox   235

All materials from the Literacy Toolbox are available as editable and printable PDFs at www.wiley.com/go/coreliteracy. Use the following password: odell2016.

INTRODUCTION TO THE CORE LITERACY PROFICIENCIES: BECOMING A LITERATE PERSON

"Literacy is the ability to use printed and written information to function in society, to achieve one's goals, and to develop one's knowledge and potential."

—Definition from the National Assessment of Adult Literacy

Becoming a Literate Person: Your school and teachers are trying to help you succeed in life—and to be the best you can be at whatever you choose to do. One of the ways they are doing this is by developing your *literacy*—but what do we mean when we talk about your literacy? A dictionary might simply tell us that developing literacy means building your *skills* as a reader, thinker, and writer—but it also might tell us that literacy is *knowledge* in an area of learning that is important to you. In addition, being literate involves ways of thinking and doing things—*habits*—that a person develops over time.

Being a literate person is even more important today—in our computer-driven world—than it was in the past, no matter what you want to do:

- Go to college and become a scientist
- Be a designer, artist, musician, or chef
- Own your own business
- Develop computer applications or video games
- Work in an industry or a construction field
- Seek a career in the military
- Just want to keep up with the news of the world

You will need to be literate whatever path in school and life you choose to follow. A recent study of the reading challenges faced by people in the United States found out that the textbooks students see in their first two years of college are much more challenging than the ones they use in high school—one reason so many new college students struggle. But the study also found that technical manuals, informational websites, and even newspapers demand a high level of

reading and thinking skills as well as specialized knowledge and strategic habits—they demand literacy.

Core Literacy Proficiencies: The learning experiences you will discover in the Odell Education Program are designed to help you take control of your own literacy development and build the skills, knowledge, and habits you will need to be successful in life. They are also designed to excite your imagination and engage you in activities that are interesting and challenging.

The learning activities you will encounter will help you develop four key core literacy proficiencies. What do we mean by this term? We've already discussed the importance of *literacy*. *Core* suggests that what you will be learning is at the center—of your literacy development, your overall success in school, and your future life. The word *proficiency* is also important, because being "proficient" at something means you can do it well, can do it on your own, and have the confidence that comes with being good at something. Developing proficiency takes time, practice, and determination. However, becoming proficient is one of the great rewards of learning—whether you are learning to read closely, to play a musical instrument, or to do a difficult skateboard trick.

Literacy Proficiency Units: The core literacy proficiencies you will develop in each of four units are as follows:

1. *Reading Closely for Textual Details:* In this unit you will develop your proficiency as an *investigator of texts*. You will learn how to

- examine things closely (images, videos, websites, and texts);
- ask and use questions to guide your close examination;
- find the key details—clues—that tell you something;
- make connections among those details; and
- use those connections to develop an observation or conclusion.

2. *Making Evidence-Based Claims:* In this unit you will develop your proficiency as a *maker and prover of claims*. You will learn how to

- use the details, connections, and evidence you find in a text to form a claim—a stated conclusion—about something you have discovered;
- organize evidence from the text to support your claim and make your case;
- express and explain your claim in writing; and
- improve your writing so that others will clearly understand and appreciate your evidence-based claim—and think about the case you have made for it.

3. *Researching to Deepen Understanding:* In this unit you will develop your proficiency as a *finder and user of information*. You will learn how to

- have an inquiring mind and ask good questions;
- search for information—in texts, interviews, and on the Internet—that can help you answer your questions;
- record and organize the information you find;
- decide what is relevant and trustworthy in the sources of your information;
- come to a research-based position or solution to a problem; and
- clearly communicate what you have learned.

4. *Building Evidence-Based Arguments:* In this unit you will develop your proficiency as a *presenter of reasoned arguments*. You will learn how to

- understand the background and key aspects of an important issue;
- look at various viewpoints on the issue;
- read the arguments of others closely and thoughtfully;
- develop your own view of the issue and take a stand about it;
- make and prove your case by using sound evidence and reasoning to support it; and
- improve your writing so that others will clearly understand and appreciate your evidence-based argument—and think about the case you have made for it.

Materials to Develop Literacy Proficiency

In each of the units, you will use the supporting materials organized in this Student Edition:

Texts

Each unit includes a set of relatively short but challenging texts, which you will read, examine, and discuss.

Tools

Each unit has its own *toolbox*—a set of graphic organizers that help you think about what you are reading or writing and record your thinking so you can discuss it with others and come back to it later.

Handouts

Each unit has a set of handouts, some of which will help you understand important things you are learning and some of which will help you be successful in completing the assignments in the unit.

Literacy Skills and Academic Habits

Throughout the units you will be developing Literacy Skills and Academic Habits. You will use these skills and habits to monitor your own growth and give feedback to other students when reading, discussing, and writing. Your teacher may use them to let you know about your areas of strength and areas in which you need to improve.

LITERACY SKILLS	DESCRIPTORS
ATTENDING TO DETAILS	Identifies words, details or quotations that are important to understanding the text
DECIPHERING WORDS	Uses context and vocabulary to define unknown words and phrases
COMPREHENDING SYNTAX	Recognizes and uses sentence structures to help understand the text
INTERPRETING LANGUAGE	Understands how words are used to express ideas and perspectives
IDENTIFYING RELATIONSHIPS	Notices important connections among details, ideas, or texts
MAKING INFERENCES	Draws sound conclusions from reading and examining the text closely
SUMMARIZING	Correctly explains what the text says about the topic
QUESTIONING	Writes questions that help identify important ideas, connections and perspectives in a text
RECOGNIZING PERSPECTIVE	Identifies and explains the author's view of the text's topic
EVALUATING INFORMATION	Assesses the relevance and credibility of information in texts
DELINEATING ARGUMENTATION	Identifies and analyzes the claims, evidence, and reasoning in arguments
FORMING CLAIMS	States a meaningful conclusion that is well supported by evidence from the text
USING EVIDENCE	Uses well-chosen details from the text to support explanations Accurately paraphrases or quotes
USING LOGIC	Supports a position through a logical sequence of related claims, premises, and supporting evidence
USING LANGUAGE	Writes and speaks clearly so others can understand claims and ideas
PRESENTING DETAILS	Inserts details and quotations effectively into written or spoken explanations
ORGANIZING IDEAS	Organizes claims, supporting ideas, and evidence in a logical order
USING CONVENTIONS	Correctly uses sentence elements, punctuation, and spelling to produce clear writing
PUBLISHING	Correctly uses, formats, and cites textual evidence to support claims
REFLECTING CRITICALLY	Uses literacy concepts to discuss and evaluate personal and peer learning

ACADEMIC HABITS	DESCRIPTORS
PREPARING	Reads the text(s) closely and thinks about the questions to prepare for tasks
ENGAGING ACTIVELY	Focuses attention on the task when working individually and with others
COLLABORATING	Works well with others while participating in text-centered discussions and group activities
COMMUNICATING CLEARLY	Presents ideas and supporting evidence so others can understand them
LISTENING	Pays attention to ideas from others and takes time to think about them
GENERATING IDEAS	Generates and develops ideas, positions, products, and solutions to problems
ORGANIZING WORK	Maintains materials so that they can be used effectively and efficiently
COMPLETING TASKS	Finishes short and extended tasks by established deadlines
REVISING	Rethinks ideas and refines work based on feedback from others
UNDERSTANDING PURPOSE AND PROCESS	Understands why and how a task should be accomplished
REMAINING OPEN	Asks questions of others rather than arguing for a personal idea or opinion
QUALIFYING VIEWS	Modifies and further justifies ideas in response to thinking from others

UNIT 1

READING CLOSELY
FOR TEXTUAL DETAILS

DEVELOPING CORE LITERACY PROFICIENCIES

GRADE 7

"We reckoned now that we were at the Pole"

GOAL

In this unit you will develop your proficiency as an investigator of texts. You will learn how to do the following:

1. Examine things closely (images, videos, websites, and texts).
2. Ask and use questions to guide your close examination.
3. Find the key details—clues—that tell you something.
4. Make connections among those details.
5. Use those connections to develop an observation or conclusion.

TOPIC

In this unit, you will learn about polar exploration and read texts written by some of the most famous explorers of the North and South Poles. You will discover that the first party to reach the South Pole was actually involved in a "great race" to get there with another exploration party from a different country. You will encounter images, videos, and websites that tell you more about polar expeditions and read what are called *historical narratives*—true accounts written by explorers about their experiences. You will also read a short story that will help you feel what it might be like to try to survive in extreme cold, as explorers must do.

ACTIVITIES

You will start by examining two photo collages to develop your skills of looking closely for key details, then work on these same skills with a video and websites. When you read, the details you look for will be things such as key information or statistics, explanations, and mental pictures the author creates through images and sentences. You'll also look for important words that you need to understand because they tell you something about the topic and how the author views it. You will learn how to use questions the way an expert investigator does—in this case to dig deeply into what you are seeing or reading. Those questions will also guide the discussions you will have with other students and your teacher. From your investigation of the texts, you will come to your own understanding of the topic of polar exploration—which you will then share with others through a final written explanation and a discussion you will lead.

READING CLOSELY FOR TEXTUAL DETAILS LITERACY TOOLBOX

In *Reading Closely for Textual Details*, you will begin to build your Literacy Toolbox by learning how to use the following handouts, tools, and checklists organized in your Student Edition.

 HANDOUTS

To support your work with the texts and the tools, you will be able to use the following informational handouts:

Reading Closely Graphic

This graphic helps you understand the relationship among the various steps you will follow as you use questions to read a text closely: *approaching, questioning, analyzing, deepening, and extending.*

Guiding Questions Handout

This handout organizes a set of good, general questions to use when you are reading any text—called Guiding Questions. The questions are organized in rows that match the questioning process in the Reading Closely Graphic (*approaching, questioning, analyzing, deepening, and extending*) and also by four areas that we often pay attention to when we read a text.

Attending to Details Handout

This handout presents descriptions and examples of the kinds of details you might look for as you read a text, for example, facts and statistics, explanations of things, images and word pictures, technical terms, and so on.

Text-Based Explanation—Final Writing and Discussion Assignment

This handout will explain to you what you will be doing in the two-part final assignment for this unit: (1) writing a multiparagraph explanation of an understanding you have come to about the topic and one of the texts and (2) participating in and leading a discussion of your text and how it compares to others in the unit. The handout will also help you know what your teacher will be looking for so you can be successful on the assignments.

TOOLS

In addition to using the handouts, you will learn how to use the following tools:

Approaching the Text Tool

This two-part tool helps you prepare to read a text closely. It provides places to think about what you initially know about the text as you *approach* it—your purpose for reading, the author, publication date, and so on. It also lets you record several *questions* that you can use to do a first reading and then a rereading of the text.

Analyzing Details Tool

This four-part tool supports you in developing and using the key skills of the unit: searching for and *selecting* key details or quotations, *recording* references from the text about where you found the details and quotations, *analyzing* what those details mean to you as a reader, and *connecting* the details to form your understanding of the text.

Questioning Path Tool

This graphic organizer will provide places for you to record questions you or your teacher want to think about as you read a particular text. You will be able to record general Guiding Questions and also questions that are very specific to the text you are reading. What you record in the **Questioning Path Tool** can help you initially *approach* the text, *question* it during a first reading and investigation, *analyze* it further, *deepen* your understanding, and *extend* your reading and thinking to other questions and texts.

Model Questioning Path Tools

For each text you will read, there is a **Questioning Path Tool** that has been filled out for you with questions to frame and guide your reading. These model Questioning Paths are just starting points, and your teacher or you may prefer to develop your own paths and questions. The model paths are organized by the steps from the Reading Closely Graphic (*approaching, questioning, analyzing, deepening, and extending*) and include general Guiding Questions from the **Guiding Questions Handout** and some questions that are specific to each text and its content. You will use these model paths to guide your reading, frame your discussions with your teacher and other students, and help you when you are doing the final activities in the unit.

CHECKLIST

You will also use this checklist throughout the unit to support peer- and self-review:

Reading Closely Literacy Skills and Discussion Habits Checklist

This checklist presents and briefly describes the literacy skills and habits you will be working on during the unit. You can use it to remind you of what you are trying to learn; reflect on what you have done when reading, discussing, or writing; or give feedback to other students. Your teacher may use it to let you know about your areas of strength and areas in which you need to improve.

READING CLOSELY FOR TEXTUAL DETAILS UNIT TEXTS

AUTHOR	DATE	PUBLISHER	NOTES
Text 1: Robert Falcon Scott and Roald Amundsen (Photo Collages)			
Various	NA	Scott Polar Research Institute, University of Cambridge, National Library of Norway, and Norwegian Polar Institute	Two collages combine pictures of the British and the Norwegian expeditions, which support examining and comparing visual details.
Text 2: *The Last Expedition*, Ch. V (Explorers' Journal)			
Robert Falcon Scott	1913	Smith Elder	Journal entry from February 2, 1911, presents Scott's almost poetic impressions early in his trip to the South Pole.
Text 3: *Roald Amundsen South Pole* (Video)			
Viking River Cruises	NA	Viking River Cruises	Combines images, maps, text, and narration, to present a historical narrative about Amundsen and the Great Race to the South Pole
Text 4: Scott's Hut and the Explorer's Heritage of Antarctica (Website)			
UNESCO World Wonders Project	NA	Google Cultural Institute	Website enables students to do a virtual tour of Scott's Antarctic hut and its surrounding landscape and links to other resources.
Text 5: *The North Pole*, Ch. XXI (Historical Narrative)			
Robert Peary	1910	Frederick A. Stokes	Narrative from the first man to reach the North Pole describes the dangers and challenges of Arctic exploration.
Text 6: "To Build a Fire" (Short Story)			
Jack London	1908	*The Century Magazine*	Excerpt from the famous short story describes a man's desperate attempts to build a saving fire after plunging into frigid water
Text 7: *The South Pole*, Ch. XII (Historical Narrative)			
Roald Amundsen	1912	John Murray	Narrative recounts the days leading up to Amundsen's triumphant arrival at the Pole on December 14, 1911—and winning the Great Race.

Text 8: *Scott's Last Expedition*, Ch. XVIII (Explorer's Journal)			
Robert Falcon Scott	1913	Smith Elder	Journal entries from January 1912 communicate disappointment about arriving at the Pole—behind Amundsen
Text 9: *Scott's Last Expedition*, Ch. XX (Explorer's Journal)			
Robert Falcon Scott	1913	Smith Elder	Final journal entries from March 1912 are written in short sentences, showing Scott's weakness and desperation.
Extended Reading: *Letters*, Ch. XX (Letters)			
Robert Falcon Scott	1913	Smith Elder	Letters Scott composed in his final days provide additional evidence of his state of mind.
Extended Reading: *Voyages of Captain Scott,* Ch. IX (Secondary Historical Narrative)			
Charles Thurley	2004	Kessinger Publishing	Turley's account illustrates contrast between primary and secondary narratives. This excerpt matches the events from Text 8.
Extended Reading: A Timeline of the Exploration of Antarctica (Website)			
NA	NA	Cool Antarctica	Cool Antarctica present many educational resources about Antarctica past and present, including this time line of exploration.
Extended Reading: British Antarctic Expedition 1910–13 Gallery (Website)			
Scott Polar Research Institute	NA	University of Cambridge	Archives of more than two thousand photos from the Antarctic expeditions of Scott and Ernest Shackleton

TEXT 1

Image Set 1

Robert Falcon Scott

Image Set 2

© Norwegian Polar Institute—np001855. http://sivert.npolar.no/fotoweb/Grid.fwx

© National Library of Norway—bldsa_NPRA1482. http://www.nb.no/nbdigital/polarbilder/Amundsen/Sydpolen-Framheim/

© National Library of Norway—bldsa_SURA0055. http://www.nb.no/nbdigital/polarbilder/Amundsen/Portretter-Privatliv/

© National Library of Norway—bldsa_NPRA0525. http://www.nb.no/nbdigital/polarbilder/Amundsen/Sydpolen-polpunktet/

© National Library of Norway—bldsa_NPRA1063. http://www.nb.no/nbdigital/polarbilder/Amundsen/Sydpolen-andre_bilder/

Roald Amundsen

TEXT 2

The Last Expedition
Robert Falcon Scott , 1911
Published by Smith Elder in 1913

Excerpt: Ch. V: Depot Laying to One Tin Can

Thursday, February 2, Camp 4

So we are resting in our tents, waiting to start to-night . . .   **P1**

Last night the temperature fell to −6° after the wind dropped—today it is warm and calm.   **P2**

Impressions

5 The **seductive** folds of the sleeping-bag.   **P3**

The hiss of the **primus** and the fragrant steam of the cooker issuing from the tent ventilator.   **P4**
The small green tent and the great white road.

The whine of a dog and the neigh of our **steeds**. The driving cloud of powdered snow.   **P5**

The crunch of footsteps which break the surface crust. The wind blown **furrows**.   **P6**

10 The blue arch beneath the smoky cloud.   **P7**

seductive	primus	steeds
tempting behavior	a portable cooking stove that uses paraffin as fuel	high-spirited horses
furrows:		
narrow indents made in the ground		

The crisp ring of the ponies' hoofs and the swish of the following **sledge**.   P8

The droning conversation of the march as driver encourages or **chides** his horse. The patter of dog   P9
pads.

The gentle flutter of our canvas shelter.   P10

15 Its deep booming sound under the full force of a blizzard.   P11

The drift snow like finest flour penetrating every hole and corner—flickering up beneath one's head   P12
covering, pricking sharply as a sand blast.

The sun with blurred image peeping shyly through the wreathing drift giving pale shadowless light.   P13

The eternal silence of the great white desert. Cloudy columns of snow drift advancing from the south,   P14
20 pale yellow **wraiths**, heralding the coming storm, blotting out one by one the sharp-cut lines of the
land.

The blizzard, Nature's protest—the **crevasse,** Nature's pitfall—that grim trap for the **unwary**—no   P15
hunter could conceal his snare so perfectly—the light rippled snow bridge gives no hint or sign of the
hidden danger, its position unguessable till man or beast is floundering, clawing and struggling for
25 foothold on the brink.

The vast silence broken only by the mellow sounds of the marching column.   P16

sledge	chides	wraiths
a sled that can be pulled by animals to carry food and possessions above snow	scolds	something thin and pale, such as a stream of smoke
crevasse	**unwary**	
a deep crack or hole especially in the ice of a glacier	not careful to look out for potential danger or harm	

TEXT 3

Roald Amundsen South Pole
Viking River Cruises
Youtube

TEXT 4

Scott's Hut and the Explorers' Heritage of Antarctica
UNESCO World Wonders Project
Google Cultural Institute
World Wonders

TEXT 5

The North Pole
Robert E. Peary
Published by Frederick A. Stokes in 1910

Excerpt: Ch. XXI: Arctic Ice Sledging as It Really Is

But the pressure ridges above described are not the worst feature of the arctic ice. Far more   **P1**

troublesome and dangerous are the "leads" (the whalers' term for lanes of open water), which are

caused by the movement of the ice under the pressure of the wind and tides. These are the ever-

present nightmare of the traveler over the frozen surface of the polar ocean—on the upward journey

5 for fear that they may prevent further advance; on the return journey for fear they may cut him off

from the land and life, leaving him to wander about and starve to death on the northern side. Their

occurrence or non-occurrence is a thing impossible to **prophesy** or calculate. They open without

warning immediately ahead of the traveler, following no apparent rule or law of action. They are the

unknown quantity of the polar equation.

10 Sometimes these leads are mere cracks running through old **floes** in nearly a straight line. Sometimes **P2**

they are zigzag lanes of water just wide enough to be impossible to cross. Sometimes they are rivers

of open water from half a mile to two miles in width, stretching east and west farther than the

eye can see.

There are various ways of crossing the leads. One can go to the right or the left, with the idea of   **P3**

15 finding some place where the opposite edges of the ice are near enough together so that our long

sledges can be bridged across. Or, if there are **indications** that the lead is closing, the traveler can wait

prophesy	floes	indications
to predict	sheets of floating ice, mainly on the surface of the sea	hints

until the ice comes quite together. If it is very cold, one may wait until the ice has formed thick enough to bear the loaded sledges going at full speed. Or, one may search for a cake of ice, or hack out a cake with pickaxes, which can be used as a ferry-boat on which to transport the sledges and teams across.

20 But all these means go for **naught** when the "big lead," which marks the edge of the continental P4 shelf where it dips down into the Arctic Ocean, is in one of its tantrums, opening just wide enough to keep a continual zone of open water or impracticable young ice in the center, as occurred on our upward journey of 1906 and the never-to-be- forgotten return journey of that expedition, when this lead nearly cut us off forever from life itself.

25 A lead might have opened right through our camp, or through one of the snow igloos, when we P5 were sleeping on the surface of the polar sea. Only—it didn't.

Should the ice open across the bed platform of an igloo, and **precipitate** its inhabitants into the P6 icy water below, they would not readily drown, because of the **buoyancy** of the air inside their fur clothing. A man dropping into the water in this way might be able to scramble onto the ice and save 30 himself; but with the thermometer at 50° below zero it would not be a pleasant **contingency**.

This is the reason why I have never used a sleeping-bag when out on the polar ice. I prefer to have P7 my legs and arms free, and to be ready for any emergency at a moment's notice. I never go to sleep when out on the sea ice without my mittens on, and if I pull my arms inside my sleeves I pull my mittens in too, so as to be ready for instant action. What chance would a man in a sleeping-bag have, 35 should he suddenly wake to find himself in the water?

naught	precipitate	buoyancy
nothing, zero	to plunge especially violently or abruptly	airiness
contingency		
predicament		

The difficulties and hardships of a journey to the North Pole are too complex to be summed up in a P8
paragraph. But, briefly stated, the worst of them are: the ragged and mountainous ice over which the
traveler must journey with his heavily loaded sledges; the often terrific wind, having the impact of a
wall of water, which he must march against at times; the open leads already described, which he must
40 cross and recross, somehow; the intense cold, sometimes as low as 60° below zero, through which he
must—by fur clothing and constant activity—keep his flesh from freezing; the difficulty of dragging
out and back over the ragged and "lead" interrupted trail enough **pemmican**, biscuit, tea, condensed
milk, and liquid fuel to keep sufficient strength in his body for traveling. It was so cold much of the
time on this last journey that the brandy was frozen solid, the petroleum was white and **viscid**, and
45 the dogs could hardly be seen for the steam of their breath. The minor discomfort of building every
night our narrow and uncomfortable snow houses, and the cold bed platform of that igloo on which
we must snatch such hours of rest as the **exigencies** of our desperate **enterprise** permitted us, seem
hardly worth mentioning in comparison with the difficulties of the main proposition itself.

At times one may be obliged to march all day long facing a blinding snowstorm with the bitter wind P9
50 searching every opening in the clothing. Those among my readers who have ever been obliged to
walk for even an hour against a blizzard, with the temperature ten or twenty degrees *above* zero,
probably have keen memories of the experience. Probably they also remember how welcome was
the warm fireside of home at the end of their journey. But let them imagine tramping through such
a storm all day long, over jagged and uneven ice, with the temperature between fifteen and thirty
55 degrees *below* zero, and no shelter to look forward to at the end of the day's march excepting a
narrow and cold snow house which they would themselves be **obliged** to build in that very storm
before they could eat or rest.

pemmican	viscid	exigencies
dried meat loaf pounded into a powder, mixed with hot fat and dried fruits or berries	covered by a sticky substance	the need or requirement involved in a circumstance
enterprise	**obliged**	
a difficult or important project that is supposed to be undertaken	to make an action or request necessary	

TEXT 6

"To Build a Fire"
Jack London
Published by *The Century Magazine* in 1908

(Excerpt)

When the man had finished, he filled his pipe and took his comfortable time over a smoke. Then he   **P1**

pulled on his mittens, settled the ear-flaps of his cap firmly about his ears, and took the creek trail

up the left fork. The dog was disappointed and yearned back toward the fire. This man did not know

cold. Possibly all the generations of his ancestry had been ignorant of cold, of real cold, of cold one

5 hundred and seven degrees below freezing-point. But the dog knew; all its ancestry knew, and it had

inherited the knowledge. And it knew that it was not good to walk abroad in such fearful cold. It was

the time to lie snug in a hole in the snow and wait for a curtain of cloud to be drawn across the face

of outer space **whence** this cold came. On the other hand, there was keen **intimacy** between the

dog and the man. The one was the **toil-slave** of the other, and the only caresses it had ever received

10 were the **caresses** of the whip-lash and of harsh and **menacing** throat-sounds that threatened the

whip-lash. So the dog made no effort to communicate its **apprehension** to the man. It was not

concerned in the welfare of the man; it was for its own sake that it **yearned** back toward the fire. But

the man whistled, and spoke to it with the sound of whip-lashes, and the dog swung in at the man's

heels and followed after.

whence	intimacy	toil-slave
from what place	a close relationship, usually affectionate and loving	hard and continuous work done by a person or animal controlled by a master
menacing	**apprehension**	**yearned**
something that threatens to cause evil	suspicion or caution of potential trouble	desire for something that is or appears unattainable

15 The man took a chew of tobacco and proceeded to start a new **amber** beard. Also, his moist breath   P2

quickly powdered with white his moustache, eyebrows, and lashes. There did not seem to be so

many springs on the left fork of the Henderson, and for half an hour the man saw no signs of any. And

then it happened. At a place where there were no signs, where the soft, unbroken snow seemed to

advertise solidity beneath, the man broke through. It was not deep. He wetted himself half-way to the

20 knees before he **floundered** out to the firm crust.

He was angry, and cursed his luck aloud. He had hoped to get into camp with the boys at six o'clock,   P3

and this would delay him an hour, for he would have to build a fire and dry out his foot-gear. This was

imperative at that low temperature—he knew that much; and he turned aside to the bank, which

he climbed. On top, tangled in the underbrush about the trunks of several small spruce trees, was a

25 high-water deposit of dry firewood—sticks and twigs principally, but also larger portions of seasoned

branches and fine, dry, last-year's grasses. He threw down several large pieces on top of the snow. This

served for a foundation and prevented the young flame from drowning itself in the snow it otherwise

would melt. The flame he got by touching a match to a small shred of birch-bark that he took from

his pocket. This burned even more readily than paper. Placing it on the foundation, he fed the young

30 flame with wisps of dry grass and with the tiniest dry twigs.

He worked slowly and carefully, keenly aware of his danger. Gradually, as the flame grew stronger,   P4

he increased the size of the twigs with which he fed it. He squatted in the snow, pulling the twigs out

from their entanglement in the brush and feeding directly to the flame. He knew there must be no

failure. When it is seventy-five below zero, a man must not fail in his first attempt to build a fire—that

35 is, if his feet are wet. If his feet are dry, and he fails, he can run along the trail for half a mile and restore

his circulation. But the circulation of wet and freezing feet cannot be restored by running when it is

seventy-five below. No matter how fast he runs, the wet feet will freeze the harder.

All this the man knew. The old-timer on Sulphur Creek had told him about it the previous fall, and   P5

now he was appreciating the advice. Already all sensation had gone out of his feet. To build the fire he

amber	floundered	imperative
yellowish-brown color	struggled in a clumsy manner	absolutely necessary or required

40 had been forced to remove his mittens, and the fingers had quickly gone numb. His pace of four miles

an hour had kept his heart pumping blood to the surface of his body and to all the extremities. But the

instant he stopped, the action of the pump eased down. The cold of space smote the unprotected tip

of the planet, and he, being on that unprotected tip, received the full force of the blow. The blood of

his body **recoiled** before it. The blood was alive, like the dog, and like the dog it wanted to hide away

45 and cover itself up from the fearful cold. So long as he walked four miles an hour, he pumped that

blood, willy-nilly, to the surface; but now it **ebbed** away and sank down into the **recesses** of his body.

The **extremities** were the first to feel its absence. His wet feet froze the faster, and his exposed fingers

numbed the faster, though they had not yet begun to freeze. Nose and cheeks were already freezing,

while the skin of all his body chilled as it lost its blood.

50 But he was safe. Toes and nose and cheeks would be only touched by the frost, for the fire was   P6

beginning to burn with strength. He was feeding it with twigs the size of his finger. In another minute

he would be able to feed it with branches the size of his wrist, and then he could remove his wet

foot-gear, and, while it dried, he could keep his naked feet warm by the fire, rubbing them at first, of

course, with snow. The fire was a success. He was safe. He remembered the advice of the old-timer

55 on Sulphur Creek, and smiled. The old-timer had been very serious in laying down the law that no

man must travel alone in the Klondike after fifty below. Well, here he was; he had had the accident;

he was alone; and he had saved himself. Those old-timers were rather womanish, some of them, he

thought. All a man had to do was to keep his head, and he was all right. Any man who was a man

could travel alone. But it was surprising, the **rapidity** with which his cheeks and nose were freezing.

60 And he had not thought his fingers could go lifeless in so short a time. Lifeless they were, for he could

scarcely make them move together to grip a twig, and they seemed remote from his body and from

him. When he touched a twig, he had to look and see whether or not he had hold of it. The wires were

pretty well down between him and his finger-ends.

recoiled	ebbed	recesses
to draw back as from alarm or disgust	flowing backward or away	secluded or inner areas or parts
extremities	**rapidity**	
the end part of a limb, as a hand or foot	swiftness; speed	

All of which counted for little. There was the fire, snapping and crackling and promising life with **P7**

65 every dancing flame. He started to untie his moccasins. They were coated with ice; the thick German

socks were like sheaths of iron half-way to the knees; and the moccasin strings were like rods of steel

all twisted and knotted as by some **conflagration**. For a moment he tugged with his numbed fingers,

then, realizing the folly of it, he drew his **sheath**-knife.

But before he could cut the strings, it happened. It was his own fault or, rather, his mistake. He **P8**

70 should not have built the fire under the spruce tree. He should have built it in the open. But it had

been easier to pull the twigs from the brush and drop them directly on the fire. Now the tree under

which he had done this carried a weight of snow on its boughs. No wind had blown for weeks, and

each bough was fully **freighted**. Each time he had pulled a twig he had communicated a slight

agitation to the tree—an i**mperceptible** agitation, so far as he was concerned, but an agitation

75 sufficient to bring about the disaster. High up in the tree one bough capsized its load of snow. This

fell on the boughs beneath, **capsizing** them. This process continued, spreading out and involving the

whole tree. It grew like an avalanche, and it descended without warning upon the man and the fire,

and the fire was blotted out! Where it had burned was a mantle of fresh and disordered snow.

The man was shocked. It was as though he had just heard his own sentence of death. For a moment **P9**

80 he sat and stared at the spot where the fire had been. Then he grew very calm.

conflagration	sheath	freighted
a large destructive fire	close-fitting covering or case	loaded; burdened
imperceptible	**capsizing**	
hidden; undetectable	to overturn or tip over accidentally	

TEXT 7

The South Pole
Roald Amundsen, 1910–1912
Published by John Murray, London, in 1912

Excerpt: Chapter XII: At the Pole

The weather did not continue fine for long. Next day (December 5) there was a gale from the   P1

north, and once more the whole plain was a mass of drifting snow. In addition to this there was

thick falling snow, which blinded us and made things worse, but a feeling of security had come

over us and helped us to advance rapidly and without hesitation, although we could see nothing.

5 That day we encountered new surface conditions—big, hard snow-waves (sastrugi). These were

anything but pleasant to work among, especially when one could not see them. It was of no use for

us "**forerunners**" to think of going in advance under these circumstances, as it was impossible to

keep on one's feet. Three or four paces was often the most we managed to do before falling down.

The sastrugi were very high, and often abrupt; if one came on them unexpectedly, one required to

10 be more than an acrobat to keep on one's feet. The plan we found to work best in these conditions

was to let Hanssen's dogs go first; this was an unpleasant job for Hanssen, and for his dogs too, but it

succeeded, and succeeded well. An upset here and there was, of course, unavoidable, but with a little

patience the sledge was always righted again. The drivers had as much as they could do to support

their sledges among these sastrugi, but while supporting the sledges, they had at the same time a

15 support for themselves. It was worse for us who had no sledges, but by keeping in the **wake** of them

we could see where the irregularities lay, and thus get over them. Hanssen deserves a special word

of praise for his driving on this surface in such weather. It is a difficult matter to drive Eskimo dogs

forward when they cannot see; but Hanssen managed it well, both getting the dogs on and steering

his course by compass . . .

forerunners	wake	
people who goes ahead or are sent in advance	the path or course left by something that has passed or gone before	

20 On the morning of December 14 the weather was of the finest, just as if it had been made for arriving **P2**

at the Pole. I am not quite sure, but I believe we **dispatched** our breakfast rather more quickly than

usual and were out of the tent sooner, though I must admit that we always accomplished this with

all reasonable **haste**. We went in the usual order—the forerunner, Hanssen, Wisting, Bjaaland, and

the **reserve** forerunner. By noon we had reached 89° 53′ by dead **reckoning**, and made ready to take

25 the rest in one stage. At 10 a.m. a light breeze had sprung up from the south-east, and it had clouded

over, so that we got no noon altitude; but the clouds were not thick, and from time to time we had a

glimpse of the sun through them. The going on that day was rather different from what it had been;

sometimes the ski went over it well, but at others it was pretty bad. We advanced that day in the

same mechanical way as before; not much was said, but eyes were used all the more. Hanssen's neck

30 grew twice as long as before in his **endeavour** to see a few inches farther. I had asked him before we

started to spy out ahead for all he was worth, and he did so with a **vengeance**. But, however keenly

he stared, he could not **descry** anything but the endless flat plain ahead of us. The dogs had dropped

their scenting, and appeared to have lost their interest in the regions about the earth's axis.

At three in the afternoon a **simultaneous** "Halt!" rang out from the drivers. They had carefully **P3**

35 examined their sledge-meters, and they all showed the full distance—our Pole by reckoning. The

goal was reached, the journey ended. I cannot say—though I know it would sound much more

effective—that the object of my life was attained. That would be romancing rather too bare-facedly. I

had better be honest and admit straight out that I have never known any man to be placed in such a

diametrically opposite position to the goal of his desires as I was at that moment. The regions around

40 the North Pole —well, yes, the North Pole itself—had attracted me from childhood, and here I was at

the South Pole. Can anything more topsy-turvy be imagined?

dispatched	haste	reserve
a method of a speedy delivery	quick action	to keep back or save for future use
reckoning	**endeavour**	**vengeance**
computation; calculation	a strenuous effort or attempt to do something difficult	great force
descry	**simultaneous**	**diametrically**
to see something that is unclear by looking closely	occurring at the same time	completely opposed; opposite

20 **Developing Core Literacy Proficiencies**

We reckoned now that we were at the Pole. Of course, every one of us knew that we were not **P4**

standing on the absolute spot; it would be an impossibility with the time and the instruments at

our disposal to **ascertain** that exact spot. But we were so near it that the few miles which possibly

45 separated us from it could not be of the slightest importance. It was our intention to make a circle

round this camp, with a radius of twelve and a half miles (20 kilometres), and to be satisfied with that.

After we had halted we collected and congratulated each other. We had good grounds for mutual

respect in what had been achieved, and I think that was just the feeling that was expressed in the firm

and powerful grasps of the fist that were exchanged.

50 After this we proceeded to the greatest and most solemn act of the whole journey—the planting of **P5**

our flag. Pride and affection shone in the five pairs of eyes that gazed upon the flag, as it unfurled

itself with a sharp crack, and waved over the Pole. I had determined that the act of planting it—the

historic event—should be equally divided among us all. It was not for one man to do this; it was for

all who had staked their lives in the struggle, and held together through thick and thin. This was the

55 only way in which I could show my gratitude to my comrades in this desolate spot. I could see that

they understood and accepted it in the spirit in which it was offered. Five weather-beaten, frost-bitten

fists they were that grasped the pole, raised the waving flag in the air, and planted it as the first at the

geographical South Pole. "Thus we plant thee, beloved flag, at the South Pole, and give to the plain on

which it lies the name of King Haakon VII.'s Plateau." That moment will certainly be remembered by all

60 of us who stood there.

ascertain		
to make certain		

TEXT 8

Scott's Last Expedition
Robert Falcon Scott, January 1912
Published by Smith Elder in 1913

Excerpt Ch. XVIII: The Summit Journey to the Pole

It is wonderful to think that two long marches would land us at the Pole. We left our depot today **P1**
with nine days' **provisions**, so that it ought to be a certain thing now, and the only **appalling**
possibility the sight of the Norwegian flag **forestalling** ours. Little Bowers continues his **indefatigable**
efforts to get good sights, and it is wonderful how he works them up in his sleeping-bag in our

5 **congested** tent. (Minimum for night −27.5°.) Only 27 miles from the Pole. We ought to do it now.

Tuesday, January 16. Camp 68. Height 9760. T. −23.5°. The worst has happened, or nearly the worst. **P2**
We marched well in the morning and covered 7 1/2 miles. Noon sight showed us in Lat. 89° 42' S., and
we started off in high spirits in the afternoon, feeling that to-morrow would see us at our destination.
About the second hour of the march Bowers' sharp eyes detected what he thought was a **cairn**; he

10 was uneasy about it, but argued that it must be a **sastrugus**. Half an hour later he detected a black
speck ahead. Soon we knew that this could not be a natural snow feature. We marched on, found that
it was a black flag tied to a sledge bearer; near by the remains of a camp; sledge tracks and ski tracks
going and coming and the clear trace of dogs' paws—many dogs. This told us the whole story. The

provisions	appalling	forestalling
supplies, especially food and other necessities	causing dismay or horror	to act beforehand with or get ahead of
indefatigable	**congested**	**cairn**
inability to become tired out	overcrowded or overburdened	a heap of stones on top of each other, used as a landmark
sastrugus		
A long wavelike ridge of snow, formed by the wind and found on the polar plains		

Developing Core Literacy Proficiencies

Norwegians have forestalled us and are first at the Pole. It is a terrible disappointment, and I am very

15 sorry for my loyal companions. Many thoughts come and much discussion have we had. Tomorrow

we must march on to the Pole and then hasten home with all the speed we can compass. All the

daydreams must go; it will be a **wearisome** return. We are **descending** in altitude—certainly also the

Norwegians found an easy way up.

Wednesday, January 17. Camp 69. T. −22° at start. Night −21°. The Pole. Yes, but under very different **P3**

20 circumstances from those expected. We have had a horrible day—add to our disappointment a head

wind 4 to 5, with a temperature −22°, and companions labouring on with cold feet and hands.

We started at 7.30, none of us having slept much after the shock of our discovery. We followed the **P4**

Norwegian sledge tracks for some way; as far as we make out there are only two men. In about three

miles we passed two small cairns. Then the weather overcast, and the tracks being increasingly drifted

25 up and obviously going too far to the west, we decided to make straight for the Pole according to

our calculations. At 12.30 Evans had such cold hands we camped for lunch—an excellent 'week-end

one.' We had marched 7.4 miles. Lat. sight gave 89° 53' 37". We started out and did 6 1/2 miles due

south. To-night little Bowers is laying himself out to get sights in terrible difficult circumstances; the

wind is blowing hard, T. −21°, and there is that curious damp, cold feeling in the air which chills one

30 to the bone in no time. We have been **descending** again, I think, but there looks to be a rise ahead;

otherwise there is very little that is different from the awful **monotony** of past days. Great God! this is

an awful place and terrible enough for us to have laboured to it without the reward of priority. Well,

it is something to have got here, and the wind may be our friend to-morrow. We have had a fat Polar

hoosh in spite of our **chagrin**, and feel comfortable inside—added a small stick of chocolate and

wearisome	descending	monotony
tiresome	to move from above to below	wearisome routine; dull and unchanging
hoosh	**chagrin**	
a thick stew made from pemmican (a mix of dried meat, fat, cereal) or other meat, biscuits, and water	a feeling of disappointment or humiliation	

35 the queer taste of a cigarette brought by Wilson. Now for the run home and a desperate struggle. I wonder if we can do it.

Thursday morning, January 18. Decided after summing up all observations that we were 3.5 miles **P5** away from the Pole—one mile beyond it and 3 to the right. More or less in this direction Bowers saw a cairn or tent.

40 We have just arrived at this tent, 2 miles from our camp, therefore about 1 1/2 miles from the Pole. **P6** In the tent we find a record of five Norwegians having been here, as follows:

Roald Amundsen

Olav Olavson Bjaaland

Hilmer Hanssen

Sverre H. Hassel

Oscar Wisting.

16 December 1911

Developing Core Literacy Proficiencies

TEXT 9

Scott's Last Expedition
Robert Falcon Scott, March 1912
Published by Smith Elder in 1913

Excerpt Ch. XX: The Last March

Friday, March 16 or Saturday 17.—Lost track of dates, but think the last correct. Tragedy all along the   **P1**
line. At lunch, the day before yesterday, poor Titus Oates said he couldn't go on; he proposed we
should leave him in his sleeping-bag. That we could not do, and **induced** him to come on, on the
afternoon march. In spite of its awful nature for him he struggled on and we made a few miles. At
5 night he was worse and we knew the end had come.

Should this be found I want these facts recorded. Oates' last thoughts were of his Mother, but   **P2**
immediately before he took pride in thinking that his **regiment** would be pleased with the bold way
in which he met his death. We can testify to his bravery. He has **borne intense** suffering for weeks
without complaint, and to the very last was able and willing to discuss outside subjects. He did not—
10 would not—give up hope to the very end. He was a brave soul. This was the end. He slept through
the night before last, hoping not to wake; but he woke in the morning—yesterday. It was blowing a
blizzard. He said, 'I am just going outside and may be some time.' He went out into the blizzard and
we have not seen him since.

I take this opportunity of saying that we have stuck to our sick companions to the last.   **P3**

induced	regiment	borne
to lead or move by persuasion or influence, as to some action or state of mind	military unit of ground forces, consisting of battalions or battle groups, headquarters, and so on	to remain constant under a heavy load
intense		
very great; a lot of		

15 In case of Edgar Evans, when absolutely out of food and he lay **insensible**, the safety of the remainder seemed to demand his **abandonment**, but Providence mercifully removed him at this critical moment. He died a natural death, and we did not leave him till two hours after his death. We knew that poor Oates was walking to his death, but though we tried to **dissuade** him, we knew it was the act of a brave man and an English gentleman. We all hope to meet the end with a similar spirit, **20** and assuredly the end is not far.

I can only write at lunch and then only occasionally. The cold is intense, −40° at midday. My   **P4** companions are unendingly cheerful, but we are all on the verge of serious frostbites, and though we constantly talk of **fetching** through I don't think anyone of us believes it in his heart.

We are cold on the march now, and at all times except meals. Yesterday we had to lay up for a   **P5** **25** blizzard and to-day we move dreadfully slowly. We are at No. 14 pony camp, only two pony marches from One Ton Depot. We leave here our **theodolite**, a camera, and Oates' sleeping-bags. Diaries, &c., and geological specimens carried at Wilson's special request, will be found with us or on our sledge.

Sunday, March 18.—To-day, lunch, we are 21 miles from the depot. Ill fortune presses, but better   **P6** may come. We have had more wind and drift from ahead yesterday; had to stop marching; wind N.W., **30** force 4, temp. −35°. No human being could face it, and we are worn out *nearly*.

My right foot has gone, nearly all the toes—two days ago I was proud possessor of best feet.   **P7** These are the steps of my downfall. Like an ass I mixed a small spoonful of curry powder with my melted pemmican—it gave me violent indigestion. I lay awake and in pain all night; woke and felt done on the march; foot went and I didn't know it. A very small measure of neglect **35** and have a foot which is not pleasant to **contemplate**. Bowers takes first place in condition,

insensible	abandonment	dissuade
unaware; unconscious	to leave something or someone	persuade not to do something
fetching	**theodolite**	**contemplate**
to go by an indirect route	precision instrument having a telescopic sight for establishing horizontal and vertical angles	think fully or deeply about

but there is not much to choose after all. The others are still confident of getting through—or pretend to be—I don't know! We have the last *half* fill of oil in our **primus** and a very small quantity of spirit—this alone between us and thirst. The wind is fair for the moment, and that is perhaps a fact to help. The mileage would have seemed ridiculously small on our outward

40 journey.

Monday, March 19.—Lunch. We camped with difficulty last night, and were dreadfully cold till after   **P8** our supper of cold pemmican and biscuit and a half a **pannikin** of cocoa cooked over the spirit. Then, **contrary** to expectation, we got warm and all slept well. To-day we started in the usual dragging manner. Sledge dreadfully heavy. We are 15 1/2 miles from the depot and ought to get there in three

45 days. What progress! We have two days' food but barely a day's fuel. All our feet are getting bad— Wilson's best, my right foot worst, left all right. There is no chance to nurse one's feet till we can get hot food into us. Amputation is the least I can hope for now, but will the trouble spread? That is the serious question. The weather doesn't give us a chance—the wind from N. to N.W. and −40° temp, today.

Wednesday, March 21.—Got within 11 miles of depot Monday night; had to lay up all yesterday in   **P9**

50 severe blizzard. To-day **forlorn** hope, Wilson and Bowers going to depot for fuel.

Thursday, March 22 and 23.—Blizzard bad as ever—Wilson and Bowers unable to start—to-morrow   **P10** last chance—no fuel and only one or two of food left—must be near the end. Have decided it shall be natural—we shall march for the depot with or without our effects and die in our tracks.

Thursday, March 29.—Since the 21st we have had a continuous **gale** from W.S.W. and S.W. We had   **P11**

55 fuel to make two cups of tea apiece and bare food for two days on the 20th. Every day we have been ready to start for our depot *11 miles* away, but outside the door of the tent it remains a scene of

primus	pannikin	contrary
a portable or fixed device that gives off heat for cooking, and so on, using coal, gas, wood	a small pan or metal cup	opposite in direction or position
forlorn	**gale**	
unhappy or miserable	very strong wind	

whirling drift. I do not think we can hope for any better things now. We shall stick it out to the end, but we are getting weaker, of course, and the end cannot be far.

It seems a pity, but I do not think I can write more.

60 **R. SCOTT.**

For God's sake look after our people.

_____

Wilson and Bowers were found in the attitude of sleep, their sleeping-bags closed over their heads   **P12**
as they would naturally close them.

65 Scott died later. He had thrown back the flaps of his sleeping-bag and opened his coat. The little wallet containing the three notebooks was under his shoulders and his arm flung across Wilson. So they were found eight months later.

_____

Inside the front cover of the third notebook were the following words: 'Diary can be read by finder   **P13**
70 to ensure recording of Records, &c., but Diary should be sent to my widow.' And on the first page:

'Send this diary to my **widow.**

'**R. SCOTT.**'

The word *wife* had been struck out and *widow* written in.

widow		
a woman whose husband has died		

Developing Core Literacy Proficiencies

EXTENDED READING

Letters
Robert Falcon Scott, 1912
Published by Smith Elder in 1913

Excerpt: Ch. XX: To Mrs. Bowers

My Dear Mrs. Bowers,

I am afraid this will reach you after one of the heaviest blows of your life. **P1**

I write when we are very near the end of our journey, and I am finishing it in company with two **P2**
gallant, noble gentlemen. One of these is your son. He had come to be one of my closest and
5 soundest friends, and I appreciate his wonderful upright nature, his ability and energy. As the troubles
have thickened his dauntless spirit ever shone brighter and he has remained cheerful, hopeful, and
indomitable to the end.

The ways of Providence are inscrutable, but there must be some reason why such a young, vigorous **P3**
and promising life is taken. My whole heart goes out in pity for you.

10 Yours,   R. SCOTT.

To the end he has talked of you and his sisters. One sees what a happy home he must have had and **P4**
perhaps it is well to look back on nothing but happiness.

He remains unselfish, self-reliant and splendidly hopeful to the end, believing in God's mercy to you. **P5**

Message to the Public

15 The causes of the disaster are not due to faulty organisation, but to misfortune in all risks which **P6**
had to be undertaken.

1. The loss of pony transport in March 1911 obliged me to start later than I had intended, and obliged **P7**
   the limits of stuff transported to be narrowed.

2. The weather throughout the outward journey, and especially the long gale in 83° S., stopped us.

20 3. The soft snow in lower reaches of glacier again reduced pace.

We fought these untoward events with a will and conquered, but it cut into our provision reserve. **P8**

Every detail of our food supplies, clothing and depôts made on the interior ice-sheet and over that **P9**
long stretch of 700 miles to the Pole and back, worked out to perfection. The advance party would
have returned to the glacier in fine form and with surplus of food, but for the astonishing failure of the
25 man whom we had least expected to fail. Edgar Evans was thought the strongest man of the party.

The Beardmore Glacier is not difficult in fine weather, but on our return we did not get a single **P10**
completely fine day; this with a sick companion enormously increased our anxieties.

As I have said else where we got into frightfully rough ice and Edgar Evans received a concussion of **P11**
the brain—he died a natural death, but left us a shaken party with the season unduly advanced.

30 But all the facts above enumerated were as nothing to the surprise which awaited us on the Barrier. **P12**
I maintain that our arrangements for returning were quite adequate, and that no one in the world
would have expected the temperatures and surfaces which we encountered at this time of the year.
On the summit in lat. 85° 86° we had −20°, −30°. On the Barrier in lat. 82°, 10,000 feet lower, we had
−30° in the day, −47° at night pretty regularly, with continuous head wind during our day marches.
35 It is clear that these circumstances come on very suddenly, and our wreck is certainly due to this
sudden advent of severe weather, which does not seem to have any satisfactory cause. I do not think
human beings ever came through such a month as we have come through, and we should have
got through in spite of the weather but for the sickening of a second companion, Captain Oates,
and a shortage of fuel in our depôts for which I cannot account, and finally, but for the storm which
40 has fallen on us within 11 miles of the depôt at which we hoped to secure our final supplies. Surely
misfortune could scarcely have exceeded this last blow. We arrived within 11 miles of our old One
Ton Camp with fuel for one last meal and food for two days. For four days we have been unable to

leave the tent—the gale howling about us. We are weak, writing is difficult, but for my own sake I do

not regret this journey, which has shown that Englishmen can endure hardships, help one another,

45 and meet death with as great a fortitude as ever in the past. We took risks, we knew we took them;

things have come out against us, and therefore we have no cause for complaint, but bow to the will

of Providence, determined still to do our best to the last. But if we have been willing to give our lives

to this enterprise, which is for the honour of our country, I appeal to our countrymen to see that those

who depend on us are properly cared for.

50 Had we lived, I should have had a tale to tell of the hardihood, endurance, and courage of my   P13

companions which would have stirred the heart of every Englishman. These rough notes and our

dead bodies must tell the tale, but surely, surely, a great rich country like ours will see that those who

are dependent on us are properly provided for.

R. SCOTT.

EXTENDED READING

The Voyages of Captain Scott
Charles Thurley
Published by Kessinger Publishing in 2004

Excerpt: Ch. IX: The South Pole

From the very beginning of the march on January 11 the pulling was heavy, but when the sun came **P1**
out the surface became as bad as bad could be. All the time the sledge rasped and creaked, and the
work of moving it onward was agonizing. At lunch-time they had managed to cover six miles but at
fearful cost to themselves, and although when they camped for the night they were only about 74
5 miles from the Pole, Scott asked himself whether they could possibly keep up such a strain for seven
more days. 'It takes it out of us like anything. None of us ever had such hard work before. . . . Our
chance still holds good if we can put the work in, but it's a terribly trying time.'

For a few minutes during the next afternoon they experienced the almost forgotten delight of having **P2**
the sledge following easily. The experience was very short but it was also very sweet, for Scott had
10 begun to fear that their powers of pulling were rapidly weakening, and those few minutes showed
him that they only wanted a good surface to get on as merrily as of old. At night they were within 63
miles of the Pole, and just longing for a better surface to help them on their way.

But whatever the condition of the surface, Bowers continued to do his work with characteristic **P3**
thoroughness and imperturbability; and after this appalling march he insisted, in spite of Scott's
15 protest, on taking sights after they had camped—an all the more remarkable display of energy as he,
being the only one of the party who pulled on foot, had spent an even more strenuous day than the
others, who had been 'comparatively restful on ski.'

Again, on the next march, they had to pull with all their might to cover some 11 miles. 'It is wearisome **P4**
work this tugging and straining to advance a light sledge. Still, we get along. I did manage to get my
20 thoughts off the work for a time to-day, which is very restful. We should be in a poor way without our
ski, though Bowers manages to struggle through the soft snow without tiring his short legs.' Sunday

Developing Core Literacy Proficiencies

night, January 14, found them at Camp 66 and less than 40 miles from the Pole. Steering was the great
difficulty on this march, because a light southerly wind with very low drift often prevented Scott from
seeing anything, and Bowers, in Scott's shadow, gave directions. By this time the feet of the whole
25 party were beginning, mainly owing to the bad condition of their finnesko, to suffer from the cold.

'Oates seems to be feeling the cold and fatigue more than the rest of us, but we are all very fit. It is a   P5
critical time, but we ought to pull through. . . . Oh! for a few fine days! So close it seems and only the
weather to balk us.'

Another terrible surface awaited them on the morrow, and they were all 'pretty well done' when   P6
30 they camped for lunch. There they decided to leave their last depot, but although their reduced load
was now very light, Scott feared that the friction would not be greatly reduced. A pleasant surprise,
however, was in store for him, as after lunch the sledge ran very lightly, and a capital march was made.
'It is wonderful,' he wrote on that night (January 15), 'to think that two long marches would land us
at the Pole. We left our depot to-day with nine days' provisions, so that it ought to be a certain thing
35 now, and the only appalling possibility the sight of the Norwegian flag forestalling ours. Little Bowers
continues his indefatigable efforts to get good sights, and it is wonderful how he works them up in his
sleeping-bag in our congested tent. Only 27 miles from the Pole. We ought to do it now.'

The next morning's march took them 7-1/2 miles nearer and their noon sight showed them in Lat. 89°   P7
42' S.; and feeling that the following day would see them at the Pole they started off after lunch in the
40 best of spirits. Then, after advancing for an hour or so, Bowers' sharp eyes detected what he thought
was a cairn, but although he was uneasy about it he argued that it must be a sastrugus.

'Half an hour later he detected a black speck ahead. Soon we knew that this could not be a natural   P8
snow feature. We marched on, found that it was a black flag tied to a sledge bearer; near by the
remains of a camp; sledge tracks and ski tracks going and coming and the clear trace of dogs' paws—
45 many dogs. This told us the whole story. The Norwegians have forestalled us and are first at the Pole.

It is a terrible disappointment, and I am very sorry for my loyal companions. Many thoughts come and   P9
much discussion have we had. To-morrow we must march on to the Pole and then hasten home with

all the speed we can compass. All the day-dreams must go; it will be a wearisome return. Certainly also the Norwegians found an easy way up.'

50 Very little sleep came to any of the party after the shock of this discovery, and when they started   P10
    at 7.30 on the next morning (January 17) head winds with a temperature of −22° added to their
    depression of spirit. For some way they followed the Norwegian tracks, and in about three miles they
    passed two cairns. Then, as the tracks became increasingly drifted up and were obviously leading
    them too far to the west, they decided to make straight for the Pole according to their calculations.
55 During the march they covered about 14 miles, and at night Scott wrote in his journal, 'The Pole. Yes,
    but under very different circumstances from those expected.'

    That announcement tells its own story, and it would be impertinent to guess at the feelings of those   P11
    intrepid travelers when they found themselves forestalled. Nevertheless they had achieved the
    purpose they had set themselves, and the fact that they could not claim the reward of priority makes
60 not one jot of difference in estimating the honours that belong to them.

    Well,' Scott continued, 'it is something to have got here, and the wind may be our friend tomorrow. . . . P12
    Now for the run home and a desperate struggle. I wonder if we can do it.'

    On the following morning after summing up all their observations, they came to the conclusion that   P13
    they were one mile beyond the Pole and three miles to the right of it, in which direction, more or less,
65 Bowers could see a tent or cairn. A march of two miles from their camp took them to the tent, in which
    they found a record of five Norwegians having been there:

    Roald Amundsen

    Olav Olavson Bjaaland

    Hilmer Hanssen

70 Sverre H. Hassel

    Oscar Wisting

EXTENDED READING

A Timeline of the Exploration of Antarctica
Cool Antarctica

British Antarctic Expedition 1910–13 Gallery
Scott Polar Research Institute
University of Cambridge

READING CLOSELY
FOR TEXTUAL DETAILS

DEVELOPING CORE LITERACY PROFICIENCIES

GRADE 7

Literacy Toolbox

ODELL
EDUCATION

READING CLOSELY GRAPHIC

1.
APPROACHING
Where do I START?
- I determine my reading purposes and take note of important information about the text.

- Why am I reading this text, and how might that influence how I approach and read it?
- What do I know (or might find out) about the text's title, author, type, publisher, publication date, and history?
- **What sequence of questions might I use to focus my reading and increase my understanding of the text?**

2.
QUESTIONING
What details do I NOTICE?
- I use questions to help me investigate important aspects of the text.

3.
ANALYZING
What do I THINK about the details?
- I question further to analyze the details I notice and determine their meaning or importance.

4.
DEEPENING
How do I deepen my UNDERSTANDING?
- I consider others' questions and develop initial observations or claims.
- I explain why and cite my evidence.

5.
EXTENDING
Where does this LEAD me?
- I pose new questions to extend my investigation of the text and topic.
- I communicate my thinking to others.

GUIDING QUESTIONS HANDOUT

1.
APPROACHING
Where do I START?

- I determine my reading purposes and take note of important information about the text.

- Why am I reading this text, and how might that influence how I approach and read it?
- What do I know (or might find out) about the text's title, author, type, publisher, publication date, and history?
- **What sequence of questions might I use to focus my reading and increase my understanding of the text?**

2.
QUESTIONING
What details do I NOTICE?

- I use questions to help me investigate important aspects of the text.

3.
ANALYZING
What do I THINK about the details?

- I question further to analyze the details I notice and determine their meaning or importance.

LANGUAGE (CCSS R.4, L.3, L.4, L.5)	IDEAS (CCSS R.2, W.3, R.8, R.9)	PERSPECTIVE (CCSS R.6)	STRUCTURE (CCSS R.5)
• What words or phrases stand out to me as powerful and important? • What do the author's words and phrases cause me to see, feel, or think? • How are key ideas, events, places, or characters described? • What unfamiliar words do I need to study or define to better understand the text?	• What do I think the text is mainly about—what is discussed in detail? • What new ideas or information do I find in the text? • Who are the main people, voices, or characters presented in the text? • What claims do I find in the text? • What ideas stand out to me as significant or interesting?	• What do I learn about the author and the purpose for writing the text? • What details or words suggest the author's perspective? • What seems to be the author's (narrator's) attitude or point of view?	• What do I notice about how the text is organized or sequenced? • What do I notice about the structure of specific elements (paragraphs, sentences, stanzas, lines, or scenes)? • In what ways does the text begin, end, and develop?
• How do specific words or phrases influence the meaning or tone of the text? • How does the author's choice of words reveal his or her purposes and perspective? • How does context define or change the meaning of key words in the text? • How does the text's language influence my understanding of important ideas or themes?	• How might I summarize the main ideas of the text and the key supporting details? • How do the text's main ideas relate to what I already know, think, or have read? • How do the main ideas, events, or people change as the text progresses? • What evidence supports the claims in the text, and what is left uncertain or unsupported?	• How does the author's perspective influence his or her presentation of ideas, themes, or arguments? • How does the author's perspective and presentation of the text compare to others? • How does the author's perspective influence my reading of the text?	• In what ways are ideas, events, and claims linked together in the text? • How do specific sections or elements of the text develop its central ideas or themes? • How does the organization of the text influence my understanding of its information, themes, or arguments?

- **What relationships do I discover among the ideas and details presented, the author's perspective, and the language or structure of the text?**

4.
DEEPENING
How do I deepen my UNDERSTANDING?

- I consider others' questions and develop initial observations or claims.
- I explain why and cite my evidence.

5.
EXTENDING
Where does this LEAD me?

- I pose new questions to extend my investigation of the text and topic.
- I communicate my thinking to others.

ODELL EDUCATION

ATTENDING TO DETAILS HANDOUT

SEARCHING FOR DETAILS

I read the text closely and mark words and phrases that help me answer my question.

As I read, I notice authors use a lot of details and strategies to develop their ideas, arguments, and narratives. Following are examples of types of details authors often use in important ways.

Author's Facts and Ideas	Author's Language and Structure	Opinions and Perspective
• Statistics	• Repeated words	• Interpretations
• Examples	• Strong language	• Explanation of ideas or events
• Vivid description	• Figurative language	• Narration
• Characters and actors	• Tone	• Personal reflection
• Events	• Organizational structure and phrases	• Beliefs

SELECTING DETAILS

I select words or phrases from my search that I think are important for answering my questions.

ANALYZING DETAILS

I reread parts of the text and think about the meaning of the details and what they tell me about my questions.

By reading closely and thinking about the details, I can make connections among them. Following are some ways details can be connected.

Facts and Ideas	Language and Structure	Opinions and Perspective
• Authors use hard facts to illustrate or define an idea.	• Authors repeat specific words or structures to emphasize meaning or tone.	• Authors compare or contrast evidence to help define their point of view.
• Authors use examples to express a belief or point of view.	• Authors use language or tone to establish a mood.	• Authors offer their explanation of ideas or events to support their beliefs.
• Authors use vivid description to compare or oppose different ideas.	• Authors use figurative language to infer emotion or embellish meaning.	• Authors tell their own story to develop their point of view.
• Authors describe different actors or characters to illustrate a comparison or contrast.	• Authors use a specific organization to enhance a point or add meaning.	• Authors use language to reveal an opinion or feeling about a topic.
• Authors use a sequence of events to arrive at a conclusion.		

ODELL EDUCATION

READING CLOSELY FINAL WRITING AND DISCUSSION TASK HANDOUT

In this unit, you have been developing your skills as an investigator of texts:

- Asking and thinking about good questions to help you examine what you read closely
- Uncovering key clues in the details, words, and information found in the texts
- Making connections among details and texts
- Discussing what you have discovered with your classmates and teacher
- Citing specific evidence from the texts to explain and support your thinking
- Recording and communicating your thinking on graphic tools and in sentences and paragraphs

Your final assignments will provide you with opportunities to use all of these related skills and to demonstrate your proficiency and growth in Reading Closely.

FINAL ASSIGNMENTS

1. **Becoming a Text Expert:** You will first become an expert about one of the three final texts in the unit. To accomplish this, you will do the following:

   a. Read and annotate the text on your own and use Guiding Questions and an *Analyzing Details Tool* to make some initial connections about the text.

   b. Compare the notes and connections you make with those made by other students who are also becoming experts about the same text.

   c. In your expert group, come up with a new text-specific question to think about when rereading the text more closely. Complete a second *Analyzing Details Tool* for this question.

   d. Study your text notes and *Analyzing Details Tools* to come up with your own central idea about the text and topic—something new you have come to understand.

   e. Think about how your text and the central idea you have discovered relates and compares to other texts in the unit.

2. **Writing a Text-Based Explanation:** On your own, you will plan and draft a multiparagraph explanation of something you have come to understand by reading and examining your text. To accomplish this, you will do the following:

   a. Present and explain the central idea you have found in the text—what you think the text is about.

   b. Use quotations and paraphrased references from the text to explain and support the central idea you are discussing.

   c. Explain how the central idea is related to what you have found out about the author's purpose in writing the text and the author's perspective on (view of) the topic.

   d. Present and explain a new understanding about the unit's topic that your text has led you to.

   e. Work with other students to review and improve your draft—and to be sure it is the best possible representation of your ideas and your skills as a reader and writer.

   f. Reflect on how well you have used Literacy Skills in developing this final explanation.

ODELL
EDUCATION

FINAL ASSIGNMENTS (Continued)

3. **Leading and Participating in a Text-Centered Discussion:** After you have become an expert about your text and written an explanation of what you understand, you will prepare for and participate in a final discussion. In this discussion, you and other students will compare your close readings of the final three texts in the unit. To accomplish this, you will do the following:

   a. Prepare a summary of what you have come to understand and written in your explanation to share with the other students in your discussion group.

   b. Reread the other two final texts so that you are prepared to discuss and compare them.

   c. Meet with your expert group to talk about your text and how to lead a discussion of it.

   d. Come up with a new question about your text that will get others to think about the connections between it and the other texts in the unit.

   e. Join a new discussion group, and share your summary about your text and the evidence you have found:

      ⇒ Point out key details to the other students in your group.

      ⇒ Explain your observations about your author's purpose and perspective.

      ⇒ Point out key words, phrases, or sentences that indicate your author's perspective.

      ⇒ Explain what you have come to understand about the topic from your text.

   f. Listen to other students' summaries and think about the connections to your text.

   g. Pose your question to the group, and lead a discussion about the three texts, asking students to present evidence from the texts that supports their thinking.

   h. Reflect on how well you have used Discussion Habits in this final discussion.

SKILLS AND HABITS TO BE DEMONSTRATED

As you become a text expert, write your text-based explanation, and participate in a text-centered discussion, think about demonstrating the Literacy Skills and Discussion Habits listed in the following to the best of your ability. Your teacher will evaluate your work and determine your grade based on how well you:

- **Attend to Details:** Identify words, details or quotations that you think are important to understanding the text.

- **Interpret Language:** Understand how words are used to express ideas and perspectives.

- **Summarize:** Correctly explain what the text says about the topic.

- **Identify Relationships:** Notice important connections among details, ideas, or texts.

- **Recognize Perspective:** Identify and explain the author's view of the text's topic.

- **Use Evidence:** Use well-chosen details from the text to support your explanation. Accurately paraphrase or quote what the author says in the text.

- **Prepare:** Read the text(s) closely and think about the questions to prepare for a text-centered discussion.

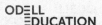

READING CLOSELY FINAL TASK HANDOUT (Continued)

SKILLS AND HABITS TO BE DEMONSTRATED (Continued)

- **Question:** Ask and respond to questions that help the discussion group understand and compare the texts.
- **Collaborate:** Pay attention to other participants while you participate in and lead a text-centered discussion.
- **Communicate Clearly:** Present your ideas and supporting evidence so others can understand them.

Note: These skills and habits are also listed on the ***Student Literacy Skills and Discussion Habits Checklist***, which you can use to assess your work and the work of other students.

ODELL
EDUCATION

READING CLOSELY FINAL TASK HANDOUT (Continued)

PART 1

UNDERSTANDING CLOSE READING

Overview and Tools

"The eternal silence of the great white desert."

OBJECTIVE:	You will learn what it means to read a text closely by paying attention to and analyzing details from the text.

MATERIALS:
- *Guiding Questions Handout*
- *Reading Closely Graphic*
- *Questioning Path Tools*

TEXTS:
- 1 Robert Falcon Scott and Roald Amundsen (Photo Collages)
- 2 *The Last Expedition*, Ch. V (Explorers' Journal)
- 3 *Roald Amundsen South Pole* (Video)
- 4 Scott's Hut and the Explorer's Heritage of Antarctica (Website)

ACTIVITIES

1. INTRODUCTION TO UNIT
Your teacher presents an overview of the unit and discusses the purposes and parts of close reading.

2. ATTENDING TO DETAILS
You explore the idea of paying attention to details through examining images.

3. READING CLOSELY FOR DETAILS
You use Guiding Questions to look closely for details in a text.

4. ATTENDING TO DETAILS IN MULTIMEDIA
You use Guiding Questions to look closely for details in a multimedia text and write a few sentences explaining something you have learned.

5. INDEPENDENT READING AND RESEARCHING ACTIVITY
You use Guiding Questions to explore a multimedia website.

QUESTIONING PATH TOOL

Text 1— Photo Collages—Polar Exploration

APPROACHING: *I determine my reading purposes and take note of key information about the text. I identify the LIPS domain(s) that will guide my initial reading.*

I will initially focus on *ideas* and supporting details.

QUESTIONING: *I use Guiding Questions to help me investigate the text (from the **Guiding Questions Handout**).*

1. What details stand out to me as I examine this collection of images? [I]

2. What do I think these images are mainly about? [I]

ANALYZING: *I question further to connect and analyze the details I find (from the **Guiding Questions Handout**).*

3. How do specific details help me understand what is being depicted in the images? [I]

DEEPENING: *I consider the questions of others.*

4. What do I notice about each of the explorers' faces? What sort of men do they appear to be?

5. What do the details of the photos suggest about the places that the men explored? Why are there flags in the photos?

6. What connections or comparisons do I notice between the two collages and the explorations they depict?

EXTENDING: *I pose my own questions.*

Example: Who were Robert Falcon Scott and Roald Amundsen? What do I think might have happened to the explorers and their expeditions?

ODELL
EDUCATION

QUESTIONING PATH TOOL

Text 2—*The Last Expedition*, Ch. V, Robert Falcon Scott

APPROACHING:
I determine my reading purposes and take note of key information about the text. I identify the LIPS domain(s) that will guide my initial reading.

I will initially note that this is a journal entry written during a 1911 exploration of Antarctica. I will first focus on its *structure* and purpose as a journal entry, then on the author's use of *language* to record his impressions of the experience.

QUESTIONING: *I use Guiding Questions to help me investigate the text (from the **Guiding Questions Handout**).*

1. What do I notice about how the text is organized or sequenced? [S]

2. What do the author's words and phrases cause me to see, feel, or think? [L]

ANALYZING: *I question further to connect and analyze the details I find (from the **Guiding Questions Handout**).*

3. What details or words suggest the author's perspective? [L/P]

DEEPENING: *I consider the questions of others.*

4. What does the organization of the text—as a series of short phrases and sentences—suggest about how the author wrote this journal entry?

5. What do the entry's first three lines tell me about what Scott is doing as he writes this journal entry? How do these details help me understand the title he gives to the entry that follows: "Impressions"?

6. Which one of Scott's short phrases stands out to me as particularly vivid—causing me to see or feel what Scott is experiencing? What other phrase offers a very different or contrasting impression?

7. Toward the end of his entry, Scott capitalizes "Nature" and then uses what words to characterize the "blizzard" and the "crevasse" as "Nature's . . ."? What do these words—and the description that follows them—suggest about how Scott views Nature?

8. How do the images and words of the final sentence of the entry contrast with the depiction of Nature that Scott presents before this final line?

EXTENDING: *I pose my own questions.*

Example: Which of Scott's contrasting "impressions" of the polar exploration—the "mellow" and peaceful or the "booming" and violent—did he experience the most as he continued his quest for the South Pole?

QUESTIONING PATH TOOL

Text 3—"Celebrating 100 Years"—Roald Amundsen Video

APPROACHING: *I determine my reading purposes and take note of key information about the text. I identify the LIPS domain(s) that will guide my initial reading.*

I will initially focus on *ideas* and supporting details. I will think about this video as a text and how it compares to print texts.

QUESTIONING: *I use Guiding Questions to help me investigate the text (from the **Guiding Questions Handout**).*

1. What new ideas or information do I find in the text (video)? [I]

2. What do I notice about how the text (video) is organized or sequenced? [S]

ANALYZING: *I question further to connect and analyze the details I find (from the **Guiding Questions Handout**).*

3. How do specific details help me understand the central ideas or themes of the text (video)? [I]

DEEPENING: *I consider the questions of others.*

4. What specific details do I learn about Roald Amundsen as an explorer, and his race to the South Pole with Robert Falcon Scott?

5. What details from the video suggest how difficult it was to survive the journey to the Pole?

6. Why might Amundsen say, "it was like being a boy again" to reach the Pole first? How do these words convey his perspective on the expedition?

7. At the end of the video, what does Amundsen seem to mean when he says, "Victory awaits him, who has everything in order. Luck we call it."?

8. What does he then suggest when he says, "Defeat is definitely due for him, who has neglected to take the necessary precautions. Bad luck we call it."?

EXTENDING: *I pose my own questions.*

Examples: As I read further in the narratives of Amundsen, Scott, and others, what do I want to learn about the explorers and their fates?

ODELL EDUCATION

QUESTIONING PATH TOOL

Independent Web Search

APPROACHING: *I determine my reading purposes and take note of key information about the text. I identify the LIPS domain(s) that will guide my initial reading.*

I will focus on new *ideas* and information I can bring back to the class. I will note key information about the website I visit and its author or source.

QUESTIONING: *I use Guiding Questions to help me investigate the text (from the **Guiding Questions Handout**).*

1. What do I notice about how the website is organized? [S]

2. What new ideas or information do I find on the website? [I]

ANALYZING: *I question further to connect and analyze the details I find (from the **Guiding Questions Handout**).*

3. How might I summarize the main ideas of the website and the key supporting details? [I]

DEEPENING: *I consider the questions of others.*

4. What interesting details, examples, or ideas can I find that relate to the other texts we are studying?

5. What details do I notice in the landscape surrounding Scott's hut? How might the area be different in the midst of the endless Arctic night or an intense blizzard?

6. What was Scott's name for the hut—and what does that suggest? Where was it located?

7. What equipment and supplies were left in the hut by the explorers, and how might they have been used?

EXTENDING: *I pose my own questions.*

Students might be asked to pose a question and bring back information related to their question.

PART 2

QUESTIONING TEXTS

Overview and Tools

"The bitter wind searching every opening in the clothing"

OBJECTIVE:	Use questioning paths to help you read and analyze texts.

MATERIALS:
- *Approaching Texts Tool*
- *Analyzing Details Tool*
- *Questioning Path Tools*
- *Reading Closely Graphic*
- *Guiding Questions Handout*
- *Attending to Details Handout*

TEXTS:
- 1 **Robert Falcon Scott and Roald Amundsen** (Photo Collages)
- 2 *The Last Expedition,* Ch. V (Explorers' Journal)
- 3 *Roald Amundsen South Pole* (Video)
- 4 *Scott's Hut and the Explorer's Heritage of Antarctica* (Website)
- 5 *The North Pole,* Ch. XXI (Historical Narrative)

ACTIVITIES

1. HOW SKILLFUL READERS APPROACH TEXTS
Your teacher shows the class how to use the **Approaching Texts Tool** and then you practice using it in pairs.

2. APPROACHING A NEW TEXT
You read a new text and use the **Approaching Texts Tool** to guide your reading.

3. ANALYZING TEXT WITH TEXT-SPECIFIC QUESTIONS
Your teacher shows the class how to use the **Analyzing Details Tool**.

4. POSING TEXT-SPECIFIC QUESTIONS
You think of your own Text-Specific Questions you can use to analyze the text.

5. INDEPENDENT WRITING ACTIVITY
You write a short paragraph explaining your analysis of the text and list supporting

APPROACHING TEXTS TOOL

Name _ _ _ _ _ _ _ _ _ _ _   Text _ _ _ _ _ _ _ _ _ _ _

APPROACHING THE TEXT

Before reading, I consider what my specific purposes for reading are.

What are my reading purposes?

I also take note of key information about the text.

Title:	Author:	Source/Publisher:
	Text type:	Publication date:

What do I already think or understand about the text based on this information?

QUESTIONING THE TEXT

As I read the text for the first time, I use Guiding Questions that relate to my reading purpose and focus. (*Can be taken from the Guiding Questions Handout.*)

Guiding Questions for *my first reading* of the text:

As I read I mark details on the text that relate to my Guiding Questions.

As I reread, I use questions I have about specific details that have emerged in my reading to focus my analysis and deepen my understanding.

Text-specific questions to help focus *my rereading* of the text:

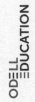

ODELL
EDUCATION

APPROACHING TEXTS TOOL

Name _____ Text _____

APPROACHING THE TEXT		
Before reading, I consider what my specific purposes for reading are.	**What are my reading purposes?**	
I also take note of key information about the text.	Title:	Source/Publisher:
	Author:	
	Text type:	Publication date:
	What do I already think or understand about the text based on this information?	

QUESTIONING THE TEXT		
As I read the text for the first time, I use Guiding Questions that relate to my reading purpose and focus. (*Can be taken from the Guiding Questions Handout.*)	**Guiding Questions for *my first reading* of the text:**	
As I reread, I use questions I have about specific details that have emerged in my reading to focus my analysis and deepen my understanding.	As I read I mark details on the text that relate to my Guiding Questions.	
	Text-specific questions to help focus *my rereading* of the text:	

ODELL
EDUCATION

QUESTIONING PATH TOOL

Text 2—The Last Expedition, Ch. V, Robert Falcon Scott

APPROACHING:
I determine my reading purposes and take note of key information about the text. I identify the LIPS domain(s) that will guide my initial reading.

I will focus on the author's use of *language* to record his impressions of the experience and convey his *perspective*.

QUESTIONING: *I use Guiding Questions to help me investigate the text (from the* **Guiding Questions Handout***).*

1. How do specific words or phrases influence the meaning or tone of the text? [L]

ANALYZING: *I question further to connect and analyze the details I find (from the* **Guiding Questions Handout***).*

2. How does the author's choice of words reveal his or her purposes and perspective? [P]

DEEPENING: *I consider the questions of others.*

3. What might Scott's presentation of contrasting images and words suggest about his impressions of and his perspective on the experiences of being an arctic explorer?

EXTENDING: *I pose my own questions.*

Example: Which of Scott's contrasting impressions of the polar exploration—the "mellow" and peaceful or the "booming" and violent—did he experience the most as he continued his quest for the South Pole?

QUESTIONING PATH TOOL

Text 5—*The North Pole*, Ch. XXI, Robert E. Peary

APPROACHING:
I determine my reading purposes and take note of key information about the text. I identify the LIPS domain(s) that will guide my initial reading.

I will initially focus on the text's *ideas* and supporting details, but I will also pay attention to its *perspective* and *language*. I will think about how knowing that the text comes from a narrative of the author's successful trip to the North Pole might influence my reading.

QUESTIONING: *I use Guiding Questions to help me investigate the text (from the **Guiding Questions Handout**).*

1. What do I think the text is mainly about—what is discussed in detail? [I]

2. What new ideas or information do I find in the text? [I]

ANALYZING: *I question further to connect and analyze the details I find (from the **Guiding Questions Handout**).*

3. What do I learn about the author and the purpose for writing the text? [P]

4. What details or words suggest the author's perspective? [P, L]

DEEPENING: *I consider the questions of others.*

5. In the first paragraph, what key words and phrases does Peary use to describe the dangers of the "leads" that arctic travelers are likely to encounter?

6. In paragraph 5, what does Peary say "might have" happened to his party, but "didn't"? What words and details does he then present in the next paragraph to describe what could happen to "a man dropping into the water in this way"?

7. In paragraph 8, what does Peary claim are some of the "worst" of the "difficulties and hardships of a journey to the North Pole"? For one of those "hardships," what do his specific descriptive words suggest about his view or perspective on polar exploration?

8. In the final paragraph, what details does Peary present to suggest the differences between his readers' experiences with blizzards and the challenges of surviving an intense storm in an arctic environment?

EXTENDING: *I pose my own questions.*

Example: How might other explorers or authors deal with or describe the hazards that Peary describes in his narrative? What might be the result if a man fell victim to one of these hazards?

ODELL
EDUCATION

APPROACHING TEXTS TOOL

Name _____ Text _____

APPROACHING THE TEXT	What are my reading purposes?
Before reading, I consider what my specific purposes for reading are.	
I also take note of key information about the text.	Author: Source/Publisher: Title: Text type: Publication date:
	What do I already think or understand about the text based on this information?

QUESTIONING THE TEXT	Guiding Questions for *my first reading* of the text:
As I read the text for the first time, I use Guiding Questions that relate to my reading purpose and focus. (*Can be taken from the Guiding Questions Handout.*)	
	As I read I mark details on the text that relate to my Guiding Questions.
As I reread, I use questions I have about specific details that have emerged in my reading to focus my analysis and deepen my understanding.	Text-specific questions to help focus *my rereading* of the text:

ODELL EDUCATION

ANALYZING DETAILS TOOL

Name - - - - - - - - - - - - - - - **Text** -

Reading purpose:

A question I have about the text:

SEARCHING FOR DETAILS | I read the text closely and mark words and phrases that help me think about my question.

SELECTING DETAILS

I select words or phrases from my search that I think are the most important in thinking about my question.

Detail 1 (Ref.:)	Detail 2 (Ref.:)	Detail 3 (Ref.:)

ANALYZING DETAILS

I reread parts of the text and think about the meaning of the details and what they tell me about my question.

What I think about detail 1:	What I think about detail 2:	What I think about detail 3:

CONNECTING DETAILS

I compare the details and explain the connections I see among them.

How I connect the details:

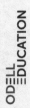

ANALYZING DETAILS TOOL

Name _ _ _ _ _ _ _ _ _ _ _ _ _ _ Text _

Reading purpose:

A question I have about the text:

SEARCHING FOR DETAILS

I read the text closely and mark words and phrases that help me think about my question.

SELECTING DETAILS

I select words or phrases from my search that I think are the most important in thinking about my question.

Detail 1 (Ref.:)	Detail 2 (Ref.:)	Detail 3 (Ref.:)

ANALYZING DETAILS

I reread parts of the text and think about the meaning of the details and what they tell me about my question.

What I think about detail 1:	What I think about detail 2:	What I think about detail 3:

CONNECTING DETAILS

I compare the details and explain the connections I see among them.

How I connect the details:

ODELL EDUCATION

ANALYZING DETAILS TOOL

Name _ _ _ _ _ _ _ _ _ _ Text _ _ _ _ _ _ _ _ _ _

Reading purpose:

A question I have about the text:

SEARCHING FOR DETAILS

I read the text closely and mark words and phrases that help me think about my question.

SELECTING DETAILS

I select words or phrases from my search that I think are the most important in thinking about my question.

Detail 1 (Ref.:)	Detail 2 (Ref.:)	Detail 3 (Ref.:)

ANALYZING DETAILS

I reread parts of the text and think about the meaning of the details and what they tell me about my question.

What I think about detail 1:	What I think about detail 2:	What I think about detail 3:

CONNECTING DETAILS

I compare the details and explain the connections I see among them.

How I connect the details:

PART 3

ANALYZING DETAILS

Overview and Tools

"It was as though he had just heard his own sentence of death."

OBJECTIVE:	You learn to analyze textual details as a key to discovering an author's perspective. You read, analyze, and compare texts.

MATERIALS:
- *Approaching Texts Tool*
- *Analyzing Details Tool*
- *Questioning Path Tools*

- *Guiding Questions Handout*
- *Reading Closely Graphic*

TEXTS:
- 1 Robert Falcon Scott and Roald Amundsen (Photo Collages)
- 2 *The Last Expedition,* Ch. V (Explorers' Journal)
- 3 *Roald Amundsen South Pole* (Video)

- 4 Scott's Hut and the Explorer's Heritage of Antarctica (Website)
- 5 *The North Pole,* Ch. XXI (Historical Narrative)
- 6 *"To Build a Fire"* (Short Story)

ACTIVITIES

1. ANALYZING TEXTUAL DETAILS
You closely read and analyze a new text.

2. ANALYZING AND DISCUSSING DETAILS ACROSS TEXTS
Your teacher guides and supports you as you compare two texts in a discussion.

3. EXPLAINING AND COMPARING TEXTS
In groups, you think about a comparative question and use the question to individually write a paragraph that compares two texts.

4. INDEPENDENT READING ACTIVITY
You independently read texts using Guiding Questions to guide your first reading.

QUESTIONING PATH TOOL

Text 6—"To Build a Fire," Jack London

APPROACHING:
I determine my reading purposes and take note of key information about the text. I identify the LIPS domain(s) that will guide my initial reading.

I will focus on the author's use of descriptive *language* and how it reveals his *perspective*. I will think about how the author, as a writer of fiction, may be using language to dramatize the characters and events he describes.

QUESTIONING: *I use Guiding Questions to help me investigate the text (from the **Guiding Questions Handout**).*

1. What do the author's words and phrases cause me to see, feel, or think? [L]

2. How are important events or characters described? [L]

ANALYZING: *I question further to connect and analyze the details I find (from the **Guiding Questions Handout**).*

3. How does the author's choice of words reveal his purpose or perspective? [L-P]

DEEPENING: *I consider the questions of others.*

4. In the first paragraph, what does the dog know that the man doesn't? How does London use this difference and related details to compare the character of the dog to the character of the man?

5. What details in paragraphs 2–7 suggest that the dog may be right when he thinks, "this man did not know cold"?

6. What events detailed in paragraph 8 cause the man first to be "shocked" and then grow "very calm" (paragraph 9)?

7. How does the author use details and description to *foreshadow* what happens to the man?

8. Based on the details in this excerpt and the *climactic* events depicted in paragraphs 8 and 9, what is a likely ending (*denouement*) for this story?

9. How is what happens to the man an example of *irony*, especially given what the dog thinks in the first paragraph and what the man thinks in paragraph 6?

EXTENDING: *I pose my own questions.*

Example: How does what happens to the man in this fictional story make me think more or differently about the polar explorers and their real accounts of their expeditions?

ODELL EDUCATION

APPROACHING TEXTS TOOL

Name _____   Text _____

APPROACHING THE TEXT	What are my reading purposes?
Before reading, I consider what my specific purposes for reading are.	
I also take note of key information about the text.	Title:
	Author: / Source/Publisher:
	Text type: / Publication date:
	What do I already think or understand about the text based on this information?

⮕

QUESTIONING THE TEXT	Guiding Questions for *my first reading* of the text:
As I read the text for the first time, I use Guiding Questions that relate to my reading purpose and focus. (*Can be taken from the Guiding Questions Handout.*)	
	As I read I mark details on the text that relate to my Guiding Questions.
As I reread, I use questions I have about specific details that have emerged in my reading to focus my analysis and deepen my understanding.	Text-specific questions to help focus *my rereading* of the text:

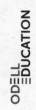

ODELL
EDUCATION

ANALYZING DETAILS TOOL

Name _____ Text _____

Reading purpose:

A question I have about the text:

SEARCHING FOR DETAILS

I read the text closely and mark words and phrases that help me think about my question.

SELECTING DETAILS

I select words or phrases from my search that I think are the most important in thinking about my question.

Detail 1 (Ref.:)	Detail 2 (Ref.:)	Detail 3 (Ref.:)

ANALYZING DETAILS

I reread parts of the text and think about the meaning of the details and what they tell me about my question.

What I think about detail 1:	What I think about detail 2:	What I think about detail 3:

CONNECTING DETAILS

I compare the details and explain the connections I see among them.

How I connect the details:

ODELL EDUCATION

ANALYZING DETAILS TOOL

Name _____ Text _____

Reading purpose:

A question I have about the text:

SEARCHING FOR DETAILS	I read the text closely and mark words and phrases that help me think about my question.		
SELECTING DETAILS I select words or phrases from my search that I think are the most important in thinking about my question.	Detail 1 (Ref.:)	Detail 2 (Ref.:)	Detail 3 (Ref.:)
ANALYZING DETAILS I reread parts of the text and think about the meaning of the details and what they tell me about my question.	What I think about detail 1:	What I think about detail 2:	What I think about detail 3:
CONNECTING DETAILS I compare the details and explain the connections I see among them.	How I connect the details:		

QUESTIONING PATH TOOL
Comparison of Text 5 and Text 6

APPROACHING:
I determine my reading purposes and take note of key information about the text. I identify the LIPS domain(s) that will guide my initial reading.

I will compare the two texts' use of *language* and details to describe the hazards of survival in Arctic conditions, and also how they reflect the author's *perspective(s)* as writers of nonfiction and fiction. Based on what I know about the two texts, I will think about the differences between historical narratives and fictional accounts.

QUESTIONING: *I use Guiding Questions to help me investigate the text (from the **Guiding Questions Handout**).*

1. What details or words suggest the author's perspective? [P-L]

ANALYZING: *I question further to connect and analyze the details I find (from the **Guiding Questions Handout**).*

2. How does the author's perspective influence the text's presentation of ideas, themes, or claims? [P]

3. How does the author's perspective and presentation of the text compare to others? [P]

DEEPENING: *I consider the questions of others.*

4. In paragraph 6, Peary says that a man "dropping into the water" at 50 degrees below zero would face an experience that "would not be a pleasant contingency." In this sentence, what does the word *contingency* mean or suggest?

5. What details does Jack London present (in paragraphs 4 and 5) to depict what the dangers of such an unforeseen event might be?

6. In what ways does each writer cause a reader to imagine the experience of trying to survive in an arctic environment?

7. Peary suggests that his readers "probably... also remember how welcome was the warm fireside of home at the end of their journey." The man in London's story briefly has a similar experience, depicted in paragraph 7: "There was the fire..." How does London describe that fire?

8. In describing what happens to the man in paragraph 8, what details does London provide that contrast sharply (and ironically) with the comforting image of the fire?

9. Robert Peary was an explorer and a scientist, and Jack London was a writer of adventure stories. How are their purposes and perspectives as writers different, and how do specific details and descriptions from their two accounts illustrate those differences?

EXTENDING: *I pose my own questions.*

Example: What are the differences in my experiences as a reader as I read these two texts? What aspects of the texts affect my different reading experiences?

ODELL EDUCATION

ANALYZING DETAILS TOOL

Name _

Text _

Reading purpose:

A question I have about the text:

SEARCHING FOR DETAILS

I read the text closely and mark words and phrases that help me think about my question.

SELECTING DETAILS

I select words or phrases from my search that I think are the most important in thinking about my question.

Detail 1 (Ref.:)	Detail 2 (Ref.:)	Detail 3 (Ref.:)

ANALYZING DETAILS

I reread parts of the text and think about the meaning of the details and what they tell me about my question.

What I think about detail 1:	What I think about detail 2:	What I think about detail 3:

CONNECTING DETAILS

I compare the details and explain the connections I see among them.

How I connect the details:

ANALYZING DETAILS TOOL

Name _ _ _ _ _ _ _ _ _ _ _ _ _ _ _ **Text** _ _ _ _ _ _ _ _ _ _ _ _ _ _ _

Reading purpose:

A question I have about the text:

SEARCHING FOR DETAILS

I read the text closely and mark words and phrases that help me think about my question.

SELECTING DETAILS

I select words or phrases from my search that I think are the most important in thinking about my question.

Detail 1 (Ref.:)	Detail 2 (Ref.:)	Detail 3 (Ref.:)

ANALYZING DETAILS

I reread parts of the text and think about the meaning of the details and what they tell me about my question.

What I think about detail 1:	What I think about detail 2:	What I think about detail 3:

CONNECTING DETAILS

I compare the details and explain the connections I see among them.

How I connect the details:

QUESTIONING PATH TOOL
Texts 7, 8, and 9

APPROACHING: *I determine my reading purposes and take note of key information about the text. I identify the LIPS domain(s) that will guide my initial reading.*

I will do a first reading of the text, thinking about the sequence of the text and events it presents, the author's use of language to describe key events, and the author's perspective on those events.

QUESTIONING: *I use Guiding Questions to help me investigate the text (from the **Guiding Questions Handout**).*

1. What do I notice about how the text is organized or sequenced? [S]

2. How are key events, places, or characters described? [L]

3. How do the text's main ideas, events, or people change as the text progresses? [I]

4. What details or words suggest the author's perspective? [P]

ANALYZING: *I question further to connect and analyze the details I find (from the **Guiding Questions Handout**).*

DEEPENING: *I consider the questions of others.*

EXTENDING: *I pose my own questions.*

APPROACHING TEXTS TOOL

Name _____ Text _____

APPROACHING THE TEXT

Before reading, I consider what my specific purposes for reading are.

What are my reading purposes?

I also take note of key information about the text.

Title:	Author:	Source/Publisher:
	Text type:	Publication date:

What do I already think or understand about the text based on this information?

QUESTIONING THE TEXT

As I read the text for the first time, I use Guiding Questions that relate to my reading purpose and focus. (Can be taken from the Guiding Questions Handout.)

Guiding Questions for *my first reading* of the text:

As I read I mark details on the text that relate to my Guiding Questions.

As I reread, I use questions I have about specific details that have emerged in my reading to focus my analysis and deepen my understanding.

Text-specific questions to help focus *my rereading* of the text:

PART 4

EXPLAINING UNDERSTANDING

Overview and Tools

"The worst has happened, or nearly the worst."

OBJECTIVE:	You learn how to summarize and explain what you have learned from reading, questioning, and analyzing texts. You read and analyze three related texts.

MATERIALS:
- *Approaching Texts Tool*
- *Analyzing Details Tool*
- *Questioning Path Tools*
- *Guiding Questions Handout*

TEXTS:
- 1 Robert Falcon Scott and Roald Amundsen (Photo Collages)
- 2 *The Last Expedition,* Ch. V (Explorers' Journal)

- 3 *Roald Amundsen South Pole* (Video)
- 4 Scott's Hut and the Explorer's Heritage of Antarctica (Website)
- 5 *The North Pole,* Ch. XXI (Historical Narrative)
- 6 *"To Build a Fire"* (Short Story)
- 7 *The South Pole,* Ch. XII (Historical Narrative)
- 8 *Scott's Last Expedition,* Ch. XVIII (Explorer's Journal)
- 9 *Scott's Last Expedition,* Ch. XX (Explorer's Journal)

☰ ACTIVITIES

1. INTRODUCTION TO CULMINATING ACTIVITIES
Your teacher introduces the final text-centered writing assignment and comparative discussion.

2. READING AND DISCUSSING RELATED TEXTS
You read three related texts and discuss them as a class.

3. QUESTIONING AND ANALYZING TEXTS INDEPENDENTLY
You select (or are assigned) one of the texts to discuss with a small group and then analyze it independently.

4. WRITING A TEXT-BASED EXPLANATION
You use your analysis to independently write a text-based explanation of one of the texts.

QUESTIONING PATH TOOL
Text 7—*The South Pole*, Ch. XII, R. Amundsen, Dec. 1911

APPROACHING:
I determine my reading purposes and take note of key information about the text. I identify the LIPS domain(s) that will guide my initial reading.

I will do a close reading of my text, looking for key details related to its *structure, language, ideas,* or *perspective,* in preparation for writing a text-based explanation and leading a comparative discussion. I will think about how the text depicts climactic events in the race for the South Pole.

QUESTIONING: *I use Guiding Questions to help me investigate the text (from the **Guiding Questions Handout**).*

1. What do I notice about how the text is organized or sequenced? [S]

2. How are key events, places, or characters described? [L]

ANALYZING: *I question further to connect and analyze the details I find (from the **Guiding Questions Handout**).*

3. How do the text's main ideas, events, or people change as the text progresses? [I]

4. What details or words suggest the author's perspective? [P]

DEEPENING: *I consider the questions of others.*

5. What is the sequence and time line of the events in Amundsen's narrative? When does the climactic event occur, and why might this be important?

6. In paragraph 1, what details does Amundsen provide to describe how challenging the final approach to the South Pole was? How do the details and the mood of paragraph 2 contrast with this opening description?

7. What do the details presented in paragraph 5 suggest about the moment of raising the first flag above the South Pole and Amundsen's view of this historic event?

8. In paragraph 3, Amundsen says, "Can anything more topsy-turvy be imagined?" What unstated ironies about his winning the race to the South Pole is he suggesting?

EXTENDING: *I pose my own questions.*

Students will develop an original question for their text in Part 4 and a comparative question in Part 5.

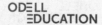
ODELL EDUCATION

QUESTIONING PATH TOOL
Text 8—*Scott's Last Expedition*, R. F. Scott, January 1912

APPROACHING:
I determine my reading purposes and take note of key information about the text. I identify the LIPS domain(s) that will guide my initial reading.

I will do a close reading of my text, looking for key details related to its *structure, language, ideas,* or *perspective,* in preparation for writing a text-based explanation and leading a comparative discussion. I will think about how the text depicts climactic events in the race for the South Pole.

QUESTIONING: *I use Guiding Questions to help me investigate the text (from the **Guiding Questions Handout**).*

1. What do I notice about how the text is organized or sequenced? [S]

2. How are key events, places, or characters described? [L]

ANALYZING: *I question further to connect and analyze the details I find (from the **Guiding Questions Handout**).*

3. How do the text's main ideas, events, or people change as the text progresses? [I]

4. What details or words suggest the author's perspective? [P]

DEEPENING: *I consider the questions of others.*

5. What is the sequence and time line of the events in Scott's journal? When does the climactic event occur, and why might this be important?

6. Scott begins his January 16 entry by saying, "The worst has happened, or nearly the worst." What details does he present in this and the next entry that let us know what his party has discovered?

7. What perspective about the expedition and emotions about its ending does Scott reveal in his January 17 entry when he says, "Great God! this is an awful place and terrible enough for us to have laboured to it without the reward of priority."?

8. When Scott presents the names of the five Norwegians that have been recorded in the tent, what does he leave unsaid about his own party and their place in history?

EXTENDING: *I pose my own questions.*

Students will develop an original question for their text in Part 4 and a comparative question in Part 5.

QUESTIONING PATH TOOL
Text 9—*Scott's Last Expedition*, R. F. Scott, March 1912

APPROACHING:
I determine my reading purposes and take note of key information about the text. I identify the LIPS domain(s) that will guide my initial reading.

I will do a close reading of my text, looking for key details related to its *structure, language, ideas,* or *perspective*, in preparation for writing a text-based explanation and leading a comparative discussion. I will think about how the text depicts climactic events in the race for the South Pole.

QUESTIONING: *I use Guiding Questions to help me investigate the text (from the **Guiding Questions Handout**).*

1. What do I notice about how the text is organized or sequenced? [S]

2. How are key events, places, or characters described? [L]

ANALYZING: *I question further to connect and analyze the details I find (from the **Guiding Questions Handout**).*

3. How do the text's main ideas, events, or people change as the text progresses? [I]

4. What details or words suggest the author's perspective? [P]

DEEPENING: *I consider the questions of others.*

5. What is the sequence and time line of the events in Scott's journal? When does the climactic event occur, and why might this be important?

6. What details recorded in Scott's journal suggest how desperate his party's situation was during the last weeks?

7. In his final entries, Scott's writing becomes very different from the writing in his earlier entries (compare these to Text 2). How are the writing and its presentation of details different? What does this change in his writing style suggest about how his perspective on his experiences has changed in his final days?

8. The details of Scott's final entries suggest that his party got within eleven miles of the supply depot before they perished. What does Scott not say about how this information might have made them feel? Why does this make his near-final words "the end cannot be far" seem very ironic?

EXTENDING: *I pose my own questions.*

Students will develop an original question for their text in Part 4 and a comparative question in Part 5.

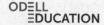

APPROACHING TEXTS TOOL

Name _ _ _ _ _ _ _ _ _ _ _ Text _ _ _ _ _ _ _ _ _ _

APPROACHING THE TEXT

Before reading, I consider what my specific purposes for reading are.

What are my reading purposes?

I also take note of key information about the text.

Title:	Author:	Source/Publisher:
	Text type:	Publication date:

What do I already think or understand about the text based on this information?

QUESTIONING THE TEXT

As I read the text for the first time, I use Guiding Questions that relate to my reading purpose and focus. (Can be taken from the Guiding Questions Handout.)

Guiding Questions for *my first reading* of the text:

As I read I mark details on the text that relate to my Guiding Questions.

As I reread, I use questions I have about specific details that have emerged in my reading to focus my analysis and deepen my understanding.

Text-specific questions to help focus *my rereading* of the text:

ODELL EDUCATION

ANALYZING DETAILS TOOL

Name _____

Text _ _ _ _ _ _ _ _ _ _ _ _ _ _ _ _

Reading purpose:

A question I have about the text:

SEARCHING FOR DETAILS

I read the text closely and mark words and phrases that help me think about my question.

SELECTING DETAILS

I select words or phrases from my search that I think are the most important in thinking about my question.

Detail 1 (Ref.:)	Detail 2 (Ref.:)	Detail 3 (Ref.:)

ANALYZING DETAILS

I reread parts of the text and think about the meaning of the details and what they tell me about my question.

What I think about detail 1:	What I think about detail 2:	What I think about detail 3:

CONNECTING DETAILS

I compare the details and explain the connections I see among them.

How I connect the details:

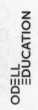

ANALYZING DETAILS TOOL

Name _____   **Text** _____

Reading purpose:

A question I have about the text:

SEARCHING FOR DETAILS

I read the text closely and mark words and phrases that help me think about my question.

SELECTING DETAILS

I select words or phrases from my search that I think are the most important in thinking about my question.

Detail 1 (Ref.:)	Detail 2 (Ref.:)	Detail 3 (Ref.:)

ANALYZING DETAILS

I reread parts of the text and think about the meaning of the details and what they tell me about my question.

What I think about detail 1:	What I think about detail 2:	What I think about detail 3:

CONNECTING DETAILS

I compare the details and explain the connections I see among them.

How I connect the details:

PART 5

DISCUSSING IDEAS

Overview and Tools

"It seems a pity, but I do not think I can write more"

OBJECTIVE:	You learn how to successfully have a text-based discussion.

MATERIALS:
- *Approaching Texts Tool*
- *Analyzing Details Tool*
- *Student Reading Closely Literacy Skills and Discussion Habits Checklist*

TEXTS:
- 1 Robert Falcon Scott and Roald Amundsen (Photo Collages)
- 2 *The Last Expedition, Ch. V* (Explorers' Journal)
- 3 Roald Amundsen South Pole (video)
- 4 Scott's Hut and the Explorer's Heritage of Antarctica (Website)
- 5 *The North Pole*, Ch. XXI (Historical Narrative)
- 6 *"To Build a Fire"* (Short Story)
- 7 *The South Pole*, Ch. XII (Historical Narrative)
- 8 *Scott's Last Expedition*, Ch. XVIII (Explorer's Journal)
- 9 *Scott's Last Expedition*, Ch. XX (Explorer's Journal)

ACTIVITIES

1. UNDERSTANDING TEXT-CENTERED DISCUSSIONS
Your teacher introduces you to productive, text-centered discussions.

2. PREPARING FOR A TEXT-CENTERED DISCUSSION
You discuss your analysis in groups and independently prepare to lead a text-centered discussion by writing down a comparative text-specific question.

3. LEADING A TEXT-CENTERED DISCUSSION
You lead and participate in text-centered discussions with other students who have analyzed different texts.

ANALYZING DETAILS TOOL

Name _ _ _ _ _ _ _ _ _ Text _ _ _ _ _ _ _ _ _ _ _ _ _

Reading purpose:

A question I have about the text:

SEARCHING FOR DETAILS	I read the text closely and mark words and phrases that help me think about my question.		
SELECTING DETAILS I select words or phrases from my search that I think are the most important in thinking about my question.	**Detail 1 (Ref.:**)	**Detail 2 (Ref.:**)	**Detail 3 (Ref.:**)
ANALYZING DETAILS I reread parts of the text and think about the meaning of the details and what they tell me about my question.	**What I think about detail 1:**	**What I think about detail 2:**	**What I think about detail 3:**
CONNECTING DETAILS I compare the details and explain the connections I see among them.	**How I connect the details:**		

ODELL
EDUCATION

STUDENT READING CLOSELY LITERACY SKILLS AND DISCUSSION HABITS CHECKLIST

READING CLOSELY LITERACY SKILLS AND DISCUSSION HABITS	✔	EVIDENCE demonstrating the SKILLS AND HABITS
READING AND THINKING		
1. **Attending to Details:** Identifies words, details, or quotations that are important to understanding the text		
2. **Interpreting Language:** Understands how words are used to express ideas and perspectives		
3. **Summarizing:** Correctly explains what the text says about the topic		
4. **Identifying Relationships:** Notices important connections among details, ideas, or texts		
5. **Recognizing Perspective:** Identifies and explains the author's view of the text's topic		
6. **Using Evidence:** Uses well-chosen details from the text to support explanations; accurately paraphrases or quotes		
DISCUSSION		
7. Preparing: Reads the text(s) closely and thinks about the questions to prepare for a text-centered discussion		
8. Questioning: Asks and responds to questions that help the discussion group understand and compare the texts		
9. Collaborating: Pays attention to other participants while participating in and leading a text-centered discussion		
10. Communicating Clearly: Presents ideas and supporting evidence so others can understand them		
General comments:		

ODELL EDUCATION

UNIT 2

MAKING EVIDENCE-BASED CLAIMS

DEVELOPING CORE LITERACY PROFICIENCIES

GRADE 7

"We organized!"

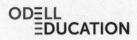

≡ GOAL

In this unit you will develop your proficiency as a maker and defender of claims. You will learn how to do the following:

1. Use the details, connections, and evidence you find in a text to form a claim—a stated conclusion—about something you have discovered.

2. Organize evidence from the text to support your claim and make your case.

3. Express and explain your claim in writing.

4. Improve your writing so that others will clearly understand and appreciate your evidence-based claim—and think about the case you have made for it.

≡ TOPIC

In this unit you will be reading and listening to three related speeches by Dr. Martin Luther King, United Farm Workers organizer Cesar Chavez, and Janet Murguia, a contemporary Hispanic leader. The three speeches all make claims about "injustice" in the United States, and they use stories from the speakers' lives as well as other information to explain and support their claims. The speeches come from different points in history—from 1968 to 2008—so you will learn how different people have viewed this issue over time. As you study the speeches, you will be learning about what a *claim* is and noting how each speaker makes claims that are based in the details of his or her own experiences. As you apply the skills from *Reading Closely for Details* of finding key details and making connections, you will take the next step as a reader and thinker. You will form your own claims that come from your reading of the texts and support them with evidence that comes from what Dr. King, Mr. Chavez, or Ms. Murguia says.

≡ ACTIVITIES

As you move through this unit from initial reading, to thinking, and to writing, the activities will help you do a close reading of short excerpts from the speeches. You will first think about what the three speakers tell their audiences and then what they seem to mean when you "read between the lines." As you learn about forming claims, you will practice finding evidence from Dr. King's speech to support a claim made by your teacher, then move on to forming your own first claims from details you notice in the speech. As you read and listen to all three speeches, you will continue to search for evidence that leads to and supports new claims. You will then learn how to organize that evidence. From this base, you will write and revise several claims, the final one a global claim about the overall meaning you have found in the speeches. You will learn to work with other students in the class to review and improve your writing so that your final claim can be as clear, strong, and evidence-based as possible.

MAKING EVIDENCE-BASED CLAIMS
LITERACY TOOLBOX

In *Making Evidence-Based Claims*, you will continue to build your "literacy toolbox" by learning how to use the following handouts, tools, and checklists organized in your Student Edition.

HANDOUTS

To support your work with the texts and the tools, you will be able to use the following informational handouts. You will also use handouts from *Reading Closely*:

Attending to Details Handout

from the *Reading Closely* unit

Guiding Questions Handout

from the *Reading Closely* unit

Writing Evidence-Based Claims Handout

This handout explains five key things you will need to think about as you write an evidence-based claim. These characteristics are also things your teacher will be looking for in the final claim you write and turn in. The handout includes examples related to one of the speeches in the unit so you can see what each of the key characteristics might look like.

Making EBCs—Final Writing Tasks Handout

This handout will explain to you what you will be doing in the final assignments for this unit: writing a multiparagraph essay that presents, explains, and uses evidence to support a claim you have formed about the meaning of one or more of the speeches you have read. The handout will also help you know what your teacher will be looking for so you can be successful on the essay assignment.

TOOLS

In addition to using the handouts, you will learn how to use the following tools. You will also apply tools from *Reading Closely*:

Approaching the Text Tool

from the *Reading Closely* unit

Analyzing Details Tool

from the *Reading Closely* unit

Questioning Path Tool

from the *Reading Closely* unit

Model Questioning Path Tools

For each section of the text you will read, there is a ***Questioning Path Tool*** that has been filled out for you to frame and guide your reading. These model Questioning Paths are just starting points, and your teacher or you may prefer to develop your own paths. The model paths are organized by the steps from the Reading Closely Graphic (approaching, questioning, analyzing, deepening, and extending). They include general Guiding Questions from the ***Guiding Questions Handout*** and some questions that are specific to each text and its content. You will use these model paths to guide your reading, frame your discussions with your teacher and other students, and help you when you are doing the final activities in the unit.

Forming Evidence-Based Claims Tool

This three-part tool will help you move in your thinking from *finding* important details, to *connecting* those details and explaining your connections, to *making a claim* based on the details and connections you have found. You can also use the tool to record evidence to support your claim and indicate where in the text you found the evidence.

Supporting Evidence-Based Claims Tool

This tool provides spaces in which you can record one or more claims about the text (either your teacher's or your own) and then quote or paraphrase supporting evidence for the claim(s)—which you will later use in organizing and writing your claim.

Organizing Evidence-Based Claims Tool

This tool provides support as you move from forming a claim and finding supporting evidence to writing the claim. The tool provides space for writing down two or three supporting points you will want to make to explain and prove your claim. Under each of these points, you can then organize the evidence you have found that relates to the point and supports your overall claim.

 CHECKLISTS

You will also use these checklists throughout the unit to support peer- and self-review:

Making Evidence-Based Claims Skills and Habits Checklists

These two checklists present and briefly describe the literacy skills and habits you will be working on during the unit. You can use the checklists to remind you of what you are trying to learn; to reflect on what you have done when reading, discussing, or writing; or to give feedback to other students. Your teacher may use them to let you know about your areas of strength and areas in which you can improve.

MAKING EVIDENCE-BASED CLAIMS
UNIT TEXTS

Excerpt of Speech Regarding the Memphis Garbage Workers Strike Delivered at Bishop Charles Mason Temple
Dr. Martin Luther King Jr.
April 3, 1968

Something is happening in Memphis; something is happening in our world. And you know, if I   P1
were standing at the beginning of time, with the possibility of taking a kind of general and
panoramic view of the whole of human history up to now, and the Almighty said to me, "Martin
Luther King, which age would you like to live in?" I would take my mental flight by Egypt and I
5   would watch God's children in their magnificent trek from the dark dungeons of Egypt through, or
rather across the Red Sea, through the wilderness on toward the promised land. And in spite of its
magnificence, I wouldn't stop there.

I would move on by Greece and take my mind to **Mount Olympus**. And I would see **Plato, Aristotle,**   P2
Socrates, Euripides and **Aristophanes** assembled around the **Parthenon**. And I would watch them
10   around the Parthenon as they discussed the great and eternal issues of reality. But I wouldn't stop there.

panoramic view	Mount Olympus	Plato, Aristotle, Socrates, Euripides, and Aristophanes
open, wide-angled view	in Greek mythology home to the Greek Gods	ancient Greek philosophers and scholars
Parthenon		
an Ancient Greek temple		

I would go on, even to the great **heyday** of the Roman Empire. And I would see developments around P3 there, through various emperors and leaders. But I wouldn't stop there.

I would even come up to the day of the **Renaissance**, and get a quick picture of all that the P4 Renaissance did for the cultural and **aesthetic** life of man. But I wouldn't stop there.

15 I would even go by the way that the man for whom I am named had his habitat. And I would watch P5 Martin Luther as he tacked his ninety-five theses on the door at the church of Wittenberg. But I wouldn't stop there. I would come on up even to 1863, and watch a **vacillating** President by the name of Abraham Lincoln finally come to the conclusion that he had to sign the Emancipation Proclamation. But I wouldn't stop there.

20 I would even come up to the early thirties, and see a man grappling with the problems of the P6 bankruptcy of his nation. And come with an **eloquent** cry that we have nothing to fear but "fear itself." But I wouldn't stop there. Strangely enough, I would turn to the Almighty, and say, "If you allow me to live just a few years in the second half of the 20th century, I will be happy."

Now that's a strange statement to make, because the world is all messed up. The nation is sick. P7
25 Trouble is in the land; confusion all around. That's a strange statement. But I know, somehow, that only when it is dark enough can you see the stars. And I see God working in this period of the twentieth century in a way that men, in some strange way, are responding. Something is happening in our world. The masses of people are rising up. And wherever they are assembled today, whether

heyday	Renaissance	aesthetic
a period of great success	a period of time between the fourteenth and seventeenth centuries; a time of cultural development from middle to modern history	relating to beauty
vacillating	**eloquent**	
changing your mind or opinions	fluent and forceful	

they are in Johannesburg, South Africa; Nairobi, Kenya; Accra, Ghana; New York City; Atlanta, Georgia;

30 Jackson, Mississippi; or Memphis, Tennessee—the cry is always the same: "We want to be free."

And another reason that I'm happy to live in this period is that we have been forced to a point where **P8**

we are going to have to **grapple** with the problems that men have been trying to grapple with

through history, but the demands didn't force them to do it. Survival demands that we grapple with

them. Men, for years now, have been talking about war and peace. But now, no longer can they just

35 talk about it. It is no longer a choice between violence and nonviolence in this world; it's nonviolence

or nonexistence. That is where we are today.

And also in the human rights revolution, if something isn't done, and done in a hurry, to bring the **P9**

colored peoples of the world out of their long years of poverty, their long years of hurt and neglect,

the whole world is doomed. Now, I'm just happy that God has allowed me to live in this period to see

40 what is unfolding. And I'm happy that He's allowed me to be in Memphis.

I can remember—I can remember when Negroes were just going around as Ralph has said, so often, **P10**

scratching where they didn't itch, and laughing when they were not tickled. But that day is all over.

We mean business now, and we are determined to gain our rightful place in God's world.

And that's all this whole thing is about. We aren't engaged in any negative protest and in any **P11**

45 negative arguments with anybody. We are saying that we are determined to be men. We are

determined to be people. We are saying—We are saying that we are God's children. And that we

are God's children, we don't have to live like we are forced to live.

Now, what does all of this mean in this great period of history? It means that we've got to stay **P12**

together. We've got to stay together and maintain **unity**. You know, whenever **Pharaoh** wanted to

50 prolong the period of slavery in Egypt, he had a favorite, favorite formula for doing it. What was that?

grapple	unity	Pharaoh
to struggle	to be in agreement, working together	ruler of ancient Egypt

He kept the slaves fighting among themselves. But whenever the slaves get together, something happens in Pharaoh's court, and he cannot hold the slaves in slavery. When the slaves get together, that's the beginning of getting out of slavery. Now let us maintain unity.

Secondly, let us keep the issues where they are. The issue is injustice. The issue is the refusal of **P13** Memphis to be fair and honest in its dealings with its public servants, who happen to be **sanitation** workers. Now, we've got to keep attention on that . . .

. . . Now we're going to march again, and we've got to march again, in order to put the issue where it **P14** is supposed to be—and force everybody to see that there are thirteen hundred of God's children here suffering, sometimes going hungry, going through dark and **dreary** nights wondering how this thing is going to come out. That's the issue. And we've got to say to the nation: We know how it's coming out. For when people get caught up with that which is right and they are willing to sacrifice for it, there is no stopping point short of victory. We aren't going to let any mace stop us. We are masters in our nonviolent movement in disarming police forces; they don't know what to do. I've seen them so often. I remember in Birmingham, Alabama, when we were in that majestic struggle there, we would move out of the 16th Street Baptist Church day after day; by the hundreds we would move out. And **Bull Connor** would tell them to send the dogs forth, and they did come; but we just went before the dogs singing, "Ain't gonna let nobody turn me around."

Bull Connor next would say, "Turn the fire hoses on." And as I said to you the other night, Bull Connor **P15** didn't know history. He knew a kind of physics that somehow didn't relate to the **transphysics** that we knew about. And that was the fact that there was a certain kind of fire that no water could put out. And we went before the fire hoses; we had known water. If we were Baptist or some other

sanitation	dreary	Bull Connor
keeping a place clean by removing waste and garbage	unpleasant, cheerless	Commissioner of Public Safety for Birmingham, Alabama, during the US civil rights movement
transphysics		
beyond the rules of physics.		

denominations, we had been **immersed**. If we were Methodist, and some others, we had been

sprinkled, but we knew water. That couldn't stop us.

And we just went on before the dogs and we would look at them; and we'd go on before the water   **P16**
75 hoses and we would look at it, and we'd just go on singing "Over my head I see freedom in the air."

And then we would be thrown in the **paddy wagons**, and sometimes we were stacked in there like

sardines in a can. And they would throw us in, and old Bull would say, "Take 'em off," and they did; and

we would just go in the paddy wagon singing, "We Shall Overcome."

And every now and then we'd get in jail, and we'd see the jailers looking through the windows being   **P17**
80 moved by our prayers, and being moved by our words and our songs. And there was a power there

which Bull Connor couldn't adjust to; and so we ended up transforming Bull into a steer, and we won

our struggle in Birmingham. Now we've got to go on in Memphis just like that. I call upon you to be

with us when we go out Monday.

Now the other thing we'll have to do is this: Always anchor our external direct action with the power   **P18**
85 of economic withdrawal. Now, we are poor people. Individually, we are poor when you compare us

with white society in America. We are poor. Never stop and forget that collectively—that means all of

us together—collectively we are richer than all the nations in the world, with the exception of nine.

Did you ever think about that?

. . . [T]he American Negro collectively is richer than most nations of the world. We have an annual   **P19**
90 income of more than thirty billion dollars a year, which is more than all of the exports of the United

States, and more than the national budget of Canada. Did you know that? That's power right there, if

we know how to **pool** it.

denominations	immersed	paddy wagons
a religious group	to be completely submerged in water	a police truck used to carry prisoners
pool		
to put everything in one place at the same time		

We don't have to argue with anybody. We don't have to curse and go around acting bad with our **P20** words. We don't need any bricks and bottles. We don't need any **Molotov cocktails**. We just need to

95 go around to these stores, and to these massive industries in our country, and say, "God sent us by here, to say to you that you're not treating his children right. And we've come by here to ask you to make the first item on your agenda fair treatment, where God's children are concerned. Now, if you are not prepared to do that, we do have an agenda that we must follow. And our agenda calls for withdrawing economic support from you." . . .

100 . . . Let me say as I move to my conclusion that we've got to give ourselves to this struggle until the end. **P21**

Nothing would be more tragic than to stop at this point in Memphis. We've got to see it through . . . **P22** Be concerned about your brother. You may not be on strike. But either we go up together, or we go down together.

Let us develop a kind of dangerous unselfishness. One day a man came to Jesus, and he wanted to **P23**

105 raise some questions about some vital matters of life. At points he wanted to trick Jesus, and show him that he knew a little more than Jesus knew and throw him off base. Now that question could have easily ended up in a philosophical and theological debate. But Jesus immediately pulled that question from mid-air, and placed it on a dangerous curve between **Jerusalem** and **Jericho**. And he talked about a certain man, who fell among thieves. You remember that a **Levite** and a priest passed by on

110 the other side.

They didn't stop to help him. And finally a man of another race came by. He got down from his beast, **P24** decided not to be compassionate **by proxy**. But he got down with him, administered first aid, and

Molotov cocktails	Jerusalem	Jericho
a breakable glass bottle containing a flammable liquid	a city in central Israel; a place of pilgrimage for Christians, Muslims, and Jews	one of the oldest cities in the world, near Jerusalem and the Jordan River
Levite	**by proxy**	
a member of the Hebrew tribe of Levi (Biblical).	the ability to do something without being physically present	

Developing Core Literacy Proficiencies

helped the man in need. Jesus ended up saying, this was the good man, this was the great man, because he had the capacity to project the "I" into the "thou," and to be concerned about his brother.

115 Now you know, we use our imagination a great deal to try to determine why the priest and the **Levite** P25 didn't stop . . .

But I'm going to tell you what my imagination tells me. It's possible that those men were afraid. You   P26 see, the Jericho road is a dangerous road. I remember when Mrs. King and I were first in Jerusalem. We rented a car and drove from Jerusalem down to Jericho. And as soon as we got on that road, I said

120 to my wife, "I can see why Jesus used this as the setting for his **parable**." It's a winding, **meandering** road. It's really conducive for ambushing. You start out in Jerusalem, which is about 1200 miles—or rather 1200 feet above sea level. And by the time you get down to Jericho, fifteen or twenty minutes later, you're about 2200 feet below sea level. That's a dangerous road. In the days of Jesus it came to be known as the "Bloody Pass."

125 And you know, it's possible that the priest and the Levite looked over that man on the ground and   P27 wondered if the robbers were still around. Or it's possible that they felt that the man on the ground was merely faking. And he was acting like he had been robbed and hurt, in order to seize them over there, **lure** them there for quick and easy seizure. And so the first question that the priest asked—the first question that the Levite asked was, "If I stop to help this man, what will happen to me?" But then

130 the Good Samaritan came by. And he reversed the question: "If I do not stop to help this man, what will happen to him?"

That's the question before you tonight. Not, "If I stop to help the sanitation workers, what will happen P28 to my job?" . . . The question is not, "If I stop to help this man in need, what will happen to me?" The question is, "If I do not stop to help the sanitation workers, what will happen to them?" That's the

135 question.

meandering	lure	
a winding course or way	to cause or persuade to go somewhere or to do something by offering something	

Let us rise up tonight with a greater readiness. Let us stand with a greater determination. And let us   **P29**

move on in these powerful days, these days of challenge to make America what it ought to be. We have

an opportunity to make America a better nation. And I want to thank God, once more, for allowing me

to be here with you. You know, several years ago, I was in New York City autographing the first book

140 that I had written. And while sitting there autographing books, a demented black woman came up.

The only question I heard from her was, "Are you Martin Luther King?" And I was looking down   **P30**

writing, and I said, "Yes." And the next minute I felt something beating on my chest. Before I knew it I

had been stabbed by this demented woman. I was rushed to Harlem Hospital. It was a dark Saturday

afternoon. And that blade had gone through, and the X-rays revealed that the tip of the blade was

145 on the edge of my **aorta,** the main **artery.** And once that's punctured, you're drowned in your own

blood—that's the end of you.

It came out in the *New York Times* the next morning, that if I had merely sneezed, I would have died.   **P31**

Well, about four days later, they allowed me, after the operation, after my chest had been opened, and

the blade had been taken out, to move around in the wheel chair in the hospital.

150 They allowed me to read some of the mail that came in, and from all over the states and the world,   **P32**

kind letters came in. I read a few, but one of them I will never forget. I had received one from the

President and the Vice-President. I've forgotten what those telegrams said. I'd received a visit and a

letter from the Governor of New York, but I've forgotten what that letter said. But there was another

letter that came from a little girl, a young girl who was a student at the White Plains High School. And I

155 looked at that letter, and I'll never forget it. It said simply,

"Dear Dr. King, I am a ninth-grade student at the White Plains High School."   **P33**

And she said,   **P34**

aorta	artery	
the main artery in the human body	a tube in the body that carries blood from the heart to the rest of the body and organs	

"While it should not matter, I would like to mention that I'm a white girl. I read in the paper of your   **P35**

misfortune, and of your suffering. And I read that if you had sneezed, you would have died. And I'm

160 simply writing you to say that I'm so happy that you didn't sneeze."

And I want to say tonight—I want to say tonight that I too am happy that I didn't sneeze. Because if   **P36**

I had sneezed, I wouldn't have been around here in 1960, when students all over the South started

sitting-in at lunch counters. And I knew that as they were sitting in, they were really standing up for the

best in the American dream, and taking the whole nation back to those great wells of democracy which

165 were dug deep by the Founding Fathers in the Declaration of Independence and the Constitution.

If I had sneezed, I wouldn't have been around here in 1961, when we decided to take a ride for   **P37**

freedom and ended segregation in inter-state travel.

If I had sneezed, I wouldn't have been around here in 1962, when Negroes in Albany, Georgia, decided **P38**

to straighten their backs up. And whenever men and women straighten their backs up, they are going

170 somewhere, because a man can't ride your back unless it is bent.

If I had sneezed—If I had sneezed I wouldn't have been here in 1963, when the black people of   **P39**

Birmingham, Alabama, aroused the conscience of this nation, and brought into being the Civil

Rights Bill.

If I had sneezed, I wouldn't have had a chance later that year, in August, to try to tell America about a   **P40**

175 dream that I had had.

If I had sneezed, I wouldn't have been down in Selma, Alabama, to see the great Movement there.   **P41**

If I had sneezed, I wouldn't have been in Memphis to see a community rally around those brothers   **P42**

and sisters who are suffering.

I'm so happy that I didn't sneeze.   **P43**

180 And they were telling me—Now, it doesn't matter, now. It really doesn't matter what happens now. I **P44**

left Atlanta this morning, and as we got started on the plane, there were six of us.

The pilot said over the public address system, "We are sorry for the delay, but we have Dr. Martin **P45**

Luther King on the plane. And to be sure that all of the bags were checked, and to be sure that

nothing would be wrong on the plane, we had to check out everything carefully. And we've had the

185 plane protected and guarded all night."

And then I got into Memphis. And some began to say the threats, or talk about the threats that were **P46**

out. What would happen to me from some of our sick white brothers?

Well, I don't know what will happen now. We've got some difficult days ahead. But it really doesn't **P47**

matter with me now, because I've been to the mountaintop. And I don't mind.

190 Like anybody, I would like to live a long life. Longevity has its place. But I'm not concerned about that **P48**

now. I just want to do God's will. And He's allowed me to go up to the mountain. And I've looked over.

And I've seen the Promised Land. I may not get there with you. But I want you to know tonight, that

we, as a people, will get to the promised land!

And so I'm happy, tonight. **P49**

195 I'm not worried about anything. **P50**

I'm not fearing any man. **P51**

Mine eyes have seen the glory of the coming of the Lord. **P52**

EXCERPT OF ADDRESS

Cesar Chavez, President of United Farm Workers of America, AFL-CIO
The Commonwealth Club of California, San Francisco
November 9, 1984

Twenty-one years ago last September, on a lonely stretch of railroad track paralleling U.S. Highway 101 near Salinas, 32 Bracero farm workers lost their lives in a tragic accident.   **P1**

The Braceros had been imported from Mexico to work on California farms. They died when their bus, which was converted from a flatbed truck, drove in front of a freight train.   **P2**

5   Conversion of the bus had not been approved by any government agency. The driver had "tunnel" vision.   **P3**

Most of the bodies lay unidentified for days. No one, including the grower who employed the workers, even knew their names.   **P4**

Today, thousands of farm workers live under **savage** conditions—beneath trees and amid garbage   **P5**
10   and human **excrement**—near tomato fields in San Diego County, tomato fields which use the most modern farm technology.

Vicious rats **gnaw** on them as they sleep. They walk miles to buy food at inflated prices. And they   **P6**
carry in water from irrigation pumps.

savage	excrement	gnaw
Brutal	solid waste from the body; feces	chew or nibble

Child labor is still common in many farm areas. **P7**

15 As much as 30 percent of Northern California's garlic harvesters are under-aged children. Kids as **P8** young as six years old have voted in state-conducted union elections since they qualified as workers.

Some 800,000 under-aged children work with their families harvesting crops across America. Babies **P9** born to migrant workers suffer 25 percent higher **infant mortality** than the rest of the population.

Malnutrition among migrant worker children is 10 times higher than the national rate. Farm **P10**
20 workers' average life expectancy is still 49 years—compared to 73 years for the average American.

All my life, I have been driven by one dream, one goal, one vision: To overthrow a farm labor system **P11** in this nation which treats farm workers as if they were not important human beings.

Farm workers are not **agricultural implements**. They are not **beasts of burden**—to be used and **P12** discarded. That dream was born in my youth. It was nurtured in my early days of organizing. It has
25 flourished. It has been attacked.

I'm not very different from anyone else who has ever tried to accomplish something with his life. My **P13** motivation comes from my personal life—from watching what my mother and father went through when I was growing up; from what we experienced as migrant farm workers in California.

That dream, that vision, grew from my own experience with racism, with hope, with the desire to be **P14**
30 treated fairly and to see my people treated as human beings and not as **chattel**.

infant mortality	malnutrition	agricultural implements
number of children that die at birth or below one year of age	the unhealthy condition that results from not eating enough food	farming equipment
beasts of burden	**chattel**	
working or farm animals that carry heavy loads	a possession; belonging to someone	

It grew from anger and rage—emotions I felt 40 years ago when people of my color were denied the   **P15**
right to see a movie or eat at a restaurant in many parts of California.

It grew from the frustration and humiliation I felt as a boy who couldn't understand how the growers   **P16**
could abuse and **exploit** farm workers when there were so many of us and so few of them.

35 Later, in the '50s, I experienced a different kind of exploitation. In San Jose, in Los Angeles and in   **P17**
other urban communities, we—the Mexican American people—were dominated by a majority that
was Anglo.

I began to realize what other minority people had discovered: That the only answer—the only hope—   **P18**
was in organizing. More of us had to become citizens. We had to register to vote. And people like me
40 had to develop the skills it would take to organize, to educate, to help empower the Chicano people.

I spent many years—before we founded the union—learning how to work with people.   **P19**

We experienced some successes in voter registration, in politics, in battling racial discrimination—   **P20**
successes in an era when Black Americans were just beginning to assert their civil rights and when
political awareness among Hispanics was almost non-existent.

45 But deep in my heart, I knew I could never be happy unless I tried organizing the farm workers. I didn't   **P21**
know if I would succeed. But I had to try.

All Hispanics—urban and rural, young and old—are connected to the farm workers' experience. We   **P22**
had all lived through the fields—or our parents had. We shared that common humiliation.

How could we progress as a people, even if we lived in the cities, while the farm workers—men and   **P23**
50 women of our color—were condemned to a life without pride?

exploit		
to take advantage of excessively		

How could we progress as a people while the farm workers—who symbolized our history in this   **P24**
land—were denied self-respect?

How could our people believe that their children could become lawyers and doctors and judges and   **P25**
business people while this shame, this injustice was permitted to continue?

55 Those who attack our union often say, 'It's not really a union. It's something else: A social movement.   **P26**
A civil rights movement. It's something dangerous."

They're half right. The United Farm Workers is first and foremost a union. A union like any other. A   **P27**
union that either produces for its members on the bread and butter issues or doesn't survive.

But the UFW has always been something more than a union—although it's never been dangerous if   **P28**
60 you believe in the Bill of Rights.

The UFW was the beginning! We attacked that historical source of shame and **infamy** that our people   **P29**
in this country lived with. We attacked that injustice, not by complaining; not by seeking hand-outs;
not by becoming soldiers in the War on Poverty.

We organized!   **P30**

65 Farm workers acknowledged we had allowed ourselves to become victims in a democratic society—a   **P31**
society where majority rule and collective bargaining are supposed to be more than academic
theories or political **rhetoric**. And by addressing this historical problem, we created confidence and
pride and hope in an entire people's ability to create the future.

union	infamy	rhetoric
a group of workers who want to achieve common goals	being well known for a negative reason	persuasive words or speech

The UFW's survival—its existence—was not in doubt in my mind when the time began to come— **P32**

70 after the union became visible—when **Chicanos** started entering college in greater numbers, when

Hispanics began running for public office in greater numbers—when our people started asserting

their rights on a broad range of issues and in many communities across the country.

The union's survival—its very existence—sent out a signal to all Hispanics that we were fighting for **P33**

our dignity, that we were challenging and overcoming injustice, that we were empowering the least

75 educated among us—the poorest among us.

The message was clear: If it could happen in the fields, it could happen anywhere—in the cities, in the **P34**

courts, in the city councils, in the state legislatures.

I didn't really appreciate it at the time, but the coming of our union signaled the start of great changes **P35**

among Hispanics that are only now beginning to be seen.

80 I've travelled to every part of this nation. I have met and spoken with thousands of Hispanics from **P36**

every walk of life—from every social and economic class.

One thing I hear most often from Hispanics, regardless of age or position—and from many non- **P37**

Hispanics as well—is that the farm workers gave them hope that they could succeed and the

inspiration to work for change . . .

85 . . . And Hispanics across California and the nation who don't work in agriculture are better off today **P38**

because of what the farm workers taught people about organization, about pride and strength, about

seizing control over their own lives.

Chicanos		
name used to refer to Mexican Americans		

Tens of thousands of the children and grandchildren of farm workers and the children and grandchildren of poor Hispanics are moving out of the fields and out of the barrios—and into the professions and into business and into politics. And that movement cannot be reversed! **P39**

Our union will forever exist as an empowering force among Chicanos in the Southwest. And that means our power and our influence will grow and not **diminish.** **P40**

Two major trends give us hope and encouragement. **P41**

First, our union has returned to a tried and tested weapon in the farm workers' non-violent arsenal—the **boycott!** . . . **P42**

. . . The other trend that gives us hope is the monumental growth of Hispanic influence in this country and what that means in increased population, increased social and economic **clout,** and increased political influence . . . **P43**

. . . In light of these trends, it is **absurd** to believe or suggest that we are going to go back in time—as a union or as a people! . . . **P44**

. . . Those politicians who ally themselves with the corporate growers and against the farm workers and the Hispanics are in for a big surprise. They want to make their careers in politics. They want to hold power 20 and 30 years from now. **P45**

But 20 and 30 years from now—in Modesto, in Salinas, in Fresno, in Bakersfield, in the Imperial Valley, and in many of the great cities of California—those communities will be dominated by farm workers **P46**

diminish	arsenal	boycott
to reduce, become less	a collection of weapons	to refuse to buy, use, or participate in (something) as a way of protesting
clout	absurd	
power, influence	ridiculous	

Developing Core Literacy Proficiencies

and not by growers, by the children and grandchildren of farm workers and not by the children and grandchildren of growers.

These trends are part of the forces of history that cannot be stopped. No person and no organization can resist them for very long. They are **inevitable.**   P47

110 Once social change begins, it cannot be reversed.   P48

You cannot uneducate the person who has learned to read. You cannot humiliate the person who feels pride. You cannot oppress the people who are not afraid anymore.   P49

Our opponents must understand that it's not just a union we have built. Unions, like other institutions, can come and go.   P50

115 But we're more than an institution. For nearly 20 years, our union has been on the cutting edge of a people's cause—and you cannot do away with an entire people; you cannot stamp out a people's cause.   P51

Regardless of what the future holds for the union, regardless of what the future holds for farm workers, our accomplishments cannot be undone. "La Causa"—our cause—doesn't have to be
120 experienced twice.   P52

The consciousness and pride that were raised by our union are alive and thriving inside millions of young Hispanics who will never work on a farm!   P53

Like the other immigrant groups, the day will come when we win the economic and political rewards which are in keeping with our numbers in society. The day will come when the politicians do the
125 right thing by our people out of political necessity and not out of charity or **idealism.**   P54

inevitable	idealism	
certain to happen	a philosophical belief of perfection not always based on reality	

That day may not come this year. That day may not come during this decade. But it will come, someday!   P55

And when that day comes, we shall see the fulfillment of that passage from the Book of Matthew in the New Testament, "That the last shall be first and the first shall be last."   P56

130   And on that day, our nation shall fulfill its **creed**—and that fulfillment shall **enrich** us all.   P57

Thank you very much.   P58

creed	enrich	
set of beliefs that guide actions	to improve	

EXCERPT OF "A SINGLE GARMENT OF DESTINY"

Janet Murguia, president and CEO National Council of La Raza
Dr. Martin Luther King, Jr. Unity Breakfast, Birmingham, Alabama
January 21, 2008

Thank you so much. It is a great pleasure to be with you today and I am truly honored to be the first **P1** Hispanic keynote speaker at the Dr. Martin Luther King, Jr. Unity Breakfast here in Birmingham . . .

. . . it is historic and visionary to recognize that Dr. King's dream was an inclusive dream and spoke to **P2** more than one community. Thank you for your courage and vision.

5 A generation has passed since my **predecessor**, Raul Yzaguirre, along with many of you in this **P3** room, marched with Dr. King to secure basic civil rights and human dignity for all Americans. That commitment to a common goal started a partnership between the newly formed National Council of *La Raza* (NCLR) and the African American civil rights movement that survives to this day. For 40 years, NCLR has stood shoulder to shoulder with the black community to promote equal opportunity for all 10 Americans.

In the 50's and 60's, the African American community showed us the way forward and swept in a **P4** wave of change to make America a better place. The Civil Rights movement helped to **liberate** all of us and moved America forward.

predecessor	liberate	
a person who had the position before you	to free	

Unit 2

99

But, for this generation, there's never been a more important time for our communities to stand together for social justice and civil rights. **P5**

15

The hate and prejudice that defined **opponents** of civil rights forty years ago has found a new home. This new strain of hate is open and ugly, and it **demonizes** all Latinos in the **emerging** debate on immigration. **P6**

The debate is needed because our immigration system is badly broken. But we must make it clear that a debate on issues is not an opportunity to dehumanize any human being. We must stop the hate. And we must do it together. **P7**

20

To quote Dr. King, "We cannot walk alone. And as we walk, we must make the pledge that we shall always march ahead. We cannot turn back." **P8**

I am here today to renew that pledge. **P9**

25 Nothing is stronger than our commitment to civil rights and human dignity. Nothing is stronger than our commitment to full and equal political participation. Nothing is stronger than our commitment to increased opportunity for all. **P10**

I am personally committed to this course and, as President of the largest national Hispanic civil rights and advocacy organization in this country, I will do everything I can to ensure that we remain united in our pursuit of a better America for all who live in this land of promise and opportunity. **P11**

30

We should note, however, that the landscape is changing. It used to be that the American Latino community was concentrated in certain cities: Houston, Los Angeles, Miami, New York and Chicago. **P12**

opponents	demonizes	emerging
people who are not in agreement	to describe (someone or something) as unpleasant or negative	increasing or growing in strength

For many years, Americans enjoyed the **fruits of our labor** and celebrated our culture, but did not see us as part of the larger American community.

35 Now, the Latino population is spreading beyond the confines of those core cities into other regions   P13
of the country. You can see it here in Birmingham. There are growing neighborhoods, businesses, retail shops and professionals where names like Rodriguez and Gomez are common.

Inevitably, with that kind of change comes tension—tension across the country and tension   P14
between our two communities. A recent survey showed that relations among African Americans,
40 Hispanics and Asian Americans are still **fraught** with misunderstandings and negative stereotypes.

And when the 2000 **census** revealed that Latinos had become the nation's largest minority group,   P15
the media and many others instantly wanted to turn it into a contest—a story about winners and losers. They wanted to create a rift between our two communities. We must not let them. We have too much in common and too much at stake.

45 But we should acknowledge that there have been tensions. They do exist. It does none of us any   P16
good, I think, to gloss over these realities. You can't solve problems by pretending they aren't there. We should discuss them, come to grips with them and move on to our much larger common agenda.

Dr. King once wrote that "I must confess that I am not afraid of the word *tension*. I have earnestly   P17
worked and preached against violent tension, but there is a constructive non-violent tension that is
50 necessary for growth.

I believe that Dr. King would want us to embrace that tension and would want us to grow together.   P18
We may come to this time and place by different paths and different journeys but we have so much in common . . . far more than those things that set us apart. We have more that unites us than divides us.

fruits of our labor	fraught	census
the results of hard work	full of (something bad or unwanted)	the official process of counting the number of people in a country

People of color are bound together by two American legacies that define our existence and frame   **P19**
55 our common struggle. One is "Hope." The other is "Hate." The conflict between them is our shared
story. One lifts us. The other restricts us. One guides us. The other divides us.

The strength of America . . . what makes it great . . . is more than the might of our armies and   **P20**
the vitality of our capital markets. It is more than the **caliber** of our educational system and the
inventiveness of our entrepreneurs. What makes America great is the "promise" of America . . . the
60 "dream" of America . . . the "hope" of America.

The African American and Hispanic community understand hope. For so long, it was all we had to   **P21**
hold onto. Hope allowed us to endure. It gave strength to our work, steel to our resolve, focus to our
ambitions and salve to our wounds. It is through hope that we shall overcome.

Dr. King saw the power in this. He saw it more clearly than the rest of us. And it was his dream that   **P22**
65 renewed us. His vision **galvanized** us. His words compelled us forward to seek the promised land.

I am a child of Dr. King's hope. I know about the power of his dream. I've seen it come true for me and   **P23**
my family. My parents, Alfredo and Amalia, came to this country more than 50 years ago with little
money and barely a grade school education.

They worked hard—my father worked in a steel plant taking all the overtime he could get and my   **P24**
70 mother took care of us kids and other kids in the neighborhood to add to the family income. We did
not have a lot of money but they sure had hope in a better tomorrow for their children. They believed
deeply in the promise of this country, especially for me and my six brothers and sisters. The values
they instilled in us—family, faith, community, education, hard work, and sacrifice—have always been
our guide.

caliber	galvanized	
a level of excellence	to cause people to become so concerned about an issue that they want to do something about it	

75 And thanks to those values and the opportunities afforded by the success of the civil rights   **P25**

movement, today, I have a brother who graduated from Harvard Law School. I also have a brother

and a sister who graduated from law school and are the first brother and sister in U.S. history to serve

on the federal bench together. And, I am very proud that my father and mother were able to visit me

when I worked in the West Wing of the White House.

80 I know the power of Dr. King's dream—I am a child of his hope—yet, I also know hate. I saw it   **P26**

throughout my youth growing up as a Latina in Kansas—I remember the pain in my father's eyes

when he would tell us about being directed to other bathrooms at work or when we were sent to

separate churches to worship. And I see it today in my work on behalf of the Latino community.

Sadly, as a nation, "hate" has defined us as well as "hope."   **P27**

85 The native peoples of this continent were nearly erased; Africans Americans were **enslaved**. Whole   **P28**

groups of people have been **exploited**, including Chinese Americans, Irish Americans and Italian

Americans. Japanese Americans were put in internment camps during WWII and, in the 1930's and

50's, thousands of people of Mexican descent—including many native-born Americans—were

deported to Mexico.

90 But, I know you know about hate. You saw it when Bull Connor unleashed the dogs and the fire   **P29**

hoses on the peaceful people here who marched in protest, singing gospel songs. You saw it again in

Albany, Georgia, again in Selma, Alabama, and again in Memphis, Tennessee.

And, of course, it was hate that took Dr. King from us . . . but, in the end, his hope was more powerful.   **P30**

His hope was our **salvation**.

enslaved	exploited	salvation
to be made a slave	to be taken advantage of	Saved

95 I come before you today, forty years later, to say our work is not done. Despite all the progress of the   P31
civil rights movement, hate has not been **vanquished**. For a time, it was beaten back. It **festered** out
of sight and away from the light.

But during the last few years, hate has found a new home.   P32

Hate is alive and well in the immigration debate. **Harbored** on the World Wide Web, hate spreads   P33
100 through the Internet unabated and unashamed and grows more **virulent** by the day.

Hate is alive and well on mainstream television, where nativist and extremist groups are called   P34
expert commentators and where media personalities grow bold and unafraid to show their prejudice.

Hate is alive and well in American politics, which has become obsessed with blaming immigrants   P35
for all of the nation's ills. They say, "Forget about health care. Forget about Iraq." They want to know,
105 "What have you done about those illegal immigrants?"...

... When presidential politicians **vie** for seeing who can be the harshest to the weakest among us, it   P36
is time for all of us to take heed.

But, politicians are not alone in embracing the hate groups and **vigilantes**. The media has offered   P37
hate a helping hand. Not only have they provided access to the airwaves to spokespeople associated
110 with hate groups, they have regularly voiced their own prejudice. Glenn Beck, a CNN commentator,
recently offered a one-stop solution to the immigration and energy crises on his radio program. He

vanquished	festered	harbored
Defeated	to become worse as time passes	kept alive
virulent	**vie**	**vigilantes**
full of hate or anger	to compete with others	people who escape the law or believe they are above it

Developing Core Literacy Proficiencies

proposed a "giant refinery" that produces "Mexinol," a fuel made from the bodies of illegal immigrants coming here from Mexico.

This kind of **vitriol** is outrageous and offensive to the Hispanic community and it is leaving an **P38**
115 **indelible** mark. Because words do matter . . . Dr. King understood the impact of words. But this kind of hate speech should offend all of us. This kind of **rhetoric** is not consistent with our American values, ideals and traditions.

It is no coincidence that in recent years, we are seeing the highest historical spike in hate crimes **P39**
against Hispanics. Hate crimes have jumped by 23 percent over the past two years, as recorded by the
120 FBI. Hate groups are growing and becoming better funded. **Nativist** extremist groups are multiplying at the local level.

The FBI has a file with my name on it. They have files with the names of my staff and the names of **P40**
NCLR Affiliates. Not because they fear us as they feared Dr. King . . . but because they fear for us . . . as targets of a growing wave of hate.

125 When hate grows, we are all **diminished**. We are all its victims. Today's struggle to defy it is just the **P41**
newest chapter in our shared history.

I ask you today to support us as we challenge those seeking office to **renounce** the politics of hate **P42**
and to distance themselves from those known to be **affiliated** with hate groups or vigilantes.

vitriol	indelible	rhetoric
harsh or angry words	impossible to remove or forget	persuasive words or speech
nativist	**diminished**	**renounce**
a person who favors native inhabitants	to become less, to reduce	to give up something or someone
affiliated		
closely connected to		

I ask you to support us today as we challenge the media to clean up their act. Hate speech has no **P43**

130 place on the air waves and those representing hate should not get a free ride to spread their agenda.

I ask you to support us today as we appeal to the American people for reason. Issues like immigration **P44** deserve serious debate and serious solutions. We cannot have that debate as long as hate has the floor.

In the 1960's, at the height of Cesar Chavez's fast to bring attention to the plight of farm workers, **P45** Dr. King sent him a telegram that read, in part: "Our separate struggles are really one. A struggle for

135 freedom, for dignity, and humanity."

Just as Dr. King supported our cause a generation ago, I ask for your support today. **P46**

From his cell in the Birmingham City Jail, Dr. King wrote, "Injustice anywhere is a threat to justice **P47** everywhere. We are caught in an inescapable network of **mutuality**, tied in a single garment of destiny. Whatever affects one directly affects all indirectly."

140 Forty years have passed since the death of Dr. King. So much has been accomplished. So much has **P48** been done. Yet, it is clear that there is so much left to do.

It is my hope that, forty years from now, we will be able to look back on this time and that historians **P49** will say that, together, we wrote a special chapter in our country's history.

That we came together and stepped up to build the **coalitions**, the bridges, the understanding that **P50**

145 allowed us to not only advance our respective communities but to move our entire nation forward.

mutuality	coalitions	
to be directly equal to	groups of people coming together for a common purpose	

For when we come together, when we passionately stand up for our principles and insist on what is right, together, we remind everyone what it means to be part of this nation of promise and of brightness . . . and of hope.   **P51**

Let us ensure that hope triumphs. We have that chance. And this is our moment.   **P52**

150 Thank you.   **P53**

MAKING
EVIDENCE-BASED CLAIMS

DEVELOPING CORE LITERACY PROFICIENCIES

GRADE 7

Literacy Toolbox

WRITING EVIDENCE-BASED CLAIMS

1. ESTABLISH THE CONTEXT

Your readers must know *where your claim is coming from* and *why it's important*. Depending on the scope of your piece and the claim, the context differs. If your whole piece is one claim or if you're introducing the first major claim of your piece, the entire context must be given:

> In his speech to the California Commonwealth Club, Cesar Chavez says . . .

Purposes of evidence-based writing vary. In some cases, naming the article and author might be enough to show why your claim is important. In other cases, you might want to give more information:

> Cesar Chavez looks ahead to see growing political and economic power for Hispanic people. In his speech to the California Commonwealth Club, Cesar Chavez says . . .

If your claim is part of a larger piece with multiple claims, then the context might be simpler:

> According to Chavez . . .   *or*   In paragraph 43, Chavez claims . . .

2. STATE YOUR CLAIM CLEARLY

How you state your claim is important; it must *clearly and fully express your ideas.* Figuring out how to state claims is a *process*. Writers revise them continually as they write their supporting evidence. Here's a claim about Chavez's speech:

> Chavez believes that Hispanic political influence in the United States will continue to grow because the positive social changes brought about by the UFW are irreversible.

Remember, you should continually return and rephrase your claim as you write the supporting evidence to make sure you are capturing exactly what you want to say. Writing out the evidence always helps you figure out what you really think.

3. ORGANIZE YOUR SUPPORTING EVIDENCE

Most claims contain multiple parts that require different evidence and should be expressed in separate paragraphs. This claim can be *broken down into two parts:*

> An explanation that *Hispanic influence will continue to grow* and an explanation that the *changes are irreversible.*

Here are two paragraphs that support the claim with evidence organized into these two parts.

WRITING EVIDENCE-BASED CLAIMS (Continued)

3. ORGANIZE YOUR SUPPORTING EVIDENCE (Continued)

An explanation that Hispanic influence will continue to grow:

Chavez believes that Hispanic political influence in the United States will continue to grow because the positive social changes brought about by the UFW are irreversible. He is full of hope and optimism at the end of his speech because he believes "monumental growth of Hispanic influence in the country . . . means an increased population, increased social and economic clout and increased political influence" (P 43). Chavez believes that because the Hispanic population is growing that politicians will have to "do the right thing . . . out of political necessity" (P 54).

An explanation that the changes are irreversible:

Chavez is also optimistic about the Hispanics' situation because the positive social changes they have experienced cannot be undone. He believes that the Hispanic peoples' situation cannot go back to the way it was because "you cannot uneducate the person who has learned to read. You cannot humiliate the person who feels pride. You cannot oppress the people who are not afraid anymore" (P 49). Chavez thinks it is impossible to reverse the changes they have made (P 39).

Notice the phrase, "Chavez is *also* . . ." starting the second paragraph. *Transitional phrases* such as this one aid the organization by showing how the ideas relate to each other.

4. PARAPHRASE AND QUOTE

Written evidence from texts can be paraphrased or quoted. It's up to the writer to decide which works better for each piece of evidence. Paraphrasing is *putting the author's words into your own.* This works well when the author originally expresses the idea you want to include across many sentences. You might write it more briefly. The last sentence in the second paragraph paraphrases the evidence from Chavez text. The ideas are his, but the exact way of writing is not.

Chavez thinks it is impossible to reverse the changes they have made (P 39).

Some evidence is better quoted than paraphrased. If an author has found the quickest way to phrase the idea or the words are especially strong, you might want to *use the author's words.* The second sentence of the second paragraph quotes Chavez exactly, incorporating his powerful phrases.

He believes that the Hispanic peoples' situation cannot go back to the way it was because "you cannot uneducate the person who has learned to read. You cannot humiliate the person who feels pride. You cannot oppress the people who are not afraid anymore" (P 49).

5. REFERENCE YOUR EVIDENCE

Whether you paraphrase or quote the author's words, you must include the *exact location where the ideas come from.* Direct quotes are written in quotation marks. How writers include the reference can vary depending on the piece and the original text. Here the writer puts the paragraph numbers from the original text in parentheses at the end of the sentence.

ODELL
EDUCATION

MAKING EVIDENCE-BASED CLAIMS
FINAL WRITING TASKS

In this unit, you have been developing your skills as a reader who can make text-based claims and prove them with evidence from the text. You have learned to do the following things:

- Uncover key clues in the details, words, and central ideas found in the texts
- Make connections among details, central ideas, and texts
- Use the details, connections, and evidence you find in texts to form a claim—a stated conclusion—about something you have discovered
- Organize evidence from the texts to support your claim and make your case
- Express and explain your claim in writing
- Improve your writing so that others will clearly understand and appreciate your evidence-based claim—and think about the case you have made for it.

Your final two writing assignments will provide you with opportunities to use all of these related skills and to demonstrate your proficiency and growth in making evidence-based claims.

FINAL ASSIGNMENTS

1. **Developing and Writing an Evidence-Based Claim:** On your own, you will read the final text in the unit closely and develop an evidence-based claim. To accomplish this, you will do the following:

   a. Read and annotate a new text (or section of text) on your own and use Guiding Questions and a *Forming EBC Tool* to develop an initial claim about the text.

   b. Compare the notes and initial claim you make with those made by other students—reframe or revise your claim.

   c. Complete an *Organizing EBC Tool* to plan subpoints and evidence you will use to explain and support your claim.

   d. Study the *Writing EBC Handout* to know what a written evidence-based claim needs to do, and what examples might look like.

   e. Draft a one- to two-paragraph written presentation and explanation of your claim, making sure that you do the things listed on the *Writing EBC Handout*:

   ⇒ Establish the context by connecting the claim to the text
   ⇒ State the claim clearly to fully communicate your ideas about the text
   ⇒ Organize supporting evidence found in the text
   ⇒ Paraphrase and quote from the text
   ⇒ Reference the evidence drawn from the text

   f. Work with other students to review and improve your draft—and to be sure it is the best possible representation of your claim and your skills as a reader and writer. Work on improving at least one of these aspects of your claim:

FINAL WRITING TASKS (Continued)

⇒ How <u>clear</u> your presentation and explanation of your claim is

⇒ How <u>defensible</u> (based on the evidence you present) your claim is

⇒ How well you have <u>presented and referenced evidence</u> to support your claim

⇒ How well you have <u>organized</u> your subpoints and evidence into a unified claim

  g. Reflect on how well you have used Literacy Skills in developing this written claim.

2. **Writing and Revising a Global or Comparative Evidence-Based Claim Essay:** On your own, you will plan and draft a multiparagraph essay that presents a global or comparative claim—one based on connections you have found among the texts (or sections of text) you have read in the unit. To accomplish this, you will do the following:

  a. Review the texts you have read, the tools you have completed, and the claims you have formed throughout the unit, looking for connections or comparisons.

  b. Use a ***Forming EBC Tool*** to make a new claim that connects or compares the texts you have read or that develops a global conclusion about the meaning of the texts.

  c. Use an ***Organizing EBC Tool*** to plan the subpoints and evidence you will use to explain and support your claim.

  d. Draft a multiparagraph essay that explains, develops, and supports your global or comparative claim—keeping in mind these three criteria for this final writing assignment. Your essay should do the following:

    ⇒ Demonstrate an accurate reading and insightful analysis of the texts you have read in the unit.

    ⇒ Develop a supported claim that is clearly connected to the content of the texts.

    ⇒ Successfully accomplish the five key elements of a written evidence-based claim (***Writing EBC Handout***).

  e. Use a collaborative process with other students to review and improve your draft in two key areas: (1) its content (quality of the claim and its evidence) and (2) its organization and expression (unity of the discussion and clarity of the writing).

  f. Reflect on how well you have used Literacy Skills in developing this final explanation.

SKILLS TO BE DEMONSTRATED

As you become a text expert and write your evidence-based claims, think about demonstrating the Literacy Skills you have been working on to the best of your ability. Your teacher will evaluate your work and determine your grade based on how well you are able to do the following things:

Read

- **Attend to Details:** Identify words, details, or quotations that you think are important to understanding the text

- **Interpret Language:** Understand how words are used to express ideas and perspectives

- **Identify Relationships:** Notice important connections among details, ideas, or texts

- **Recognize Perspective:** Identify and explain each author's view of the unit's topic

ODELL
EDUCATION

FINAL WRITING TASKS (Continued)

SKILLS TO BE DEMONSTRATED (Continued)

Think

- **Make Inferences:** Draw sound conclusions from reading and examining the texts closely
- **Form a Claim:** State a meaningful conclusion that is well supported by evidence from the texts
- **Use Evidence:** Use well-chosen details from the texts to support your claim; accurately paraphrase or quote what the authors say in the texts

Write

- **Present Details:** Insert details and quotations effectively into your essay
- **Organize Ideas:** Organize your claim, supporting ideas, and evidence in a logical order
- **Use Language:** Write clearly so others can understand your claim and supporting ideas
- **Use Conventions:** Correctly use sentence elements, punctuation, and spelling to produce clear writing
- **Publish:** Correctly use, format, and cite textual evidence to support your claim

HABITS TO BE DEVELOPED

Your teacher may also want you to reflect on how well you have used and developed the following habits of text-centered discussion when you worked with others to understand the texts and improve your writing:

- **Engage Actively:** Focus your attention on the assigned tasks when working individually and with others
- **Collaborate:** Work respectfully and productively to help your discussion or review group be successful
- **Communicate Clearly:** Present your ideas and supporting evidence so others can understand them
- **Listen:** Pay attention to ideas from others and take time to think about them
- **Understand Purpose and Process:** Understand why and how a text-centered discussion or peer writing review should be accomplished
- **Revise:** Rethink your ideas and refine your writing based on feedback from others
- **Remain Open:** Modify and further justify ideas in response to thinking from others.

Note: These skills and habits are also listed on the **Student Literacy Skills** and **Academic Habits Checklists**, which you can use to assess your work and the work of other students.

PART 1

UNDERSTANDING EVIDENCE-BASED CLAIMS

Overview and Tools

"The issue is injustice."

OBJECTIVE:	To learn about making evidence-based claims through a reading a text.

MATERIALS:
- *Guiding Questions Handout*
- *Reading Closely Graphic*
- *Questioning Path Tools*

- *Attending to Details Handout*
- *Forming EBC Tool*
- *Supporting EBC Tool*

TEXTS:
1 Martin Luther King's 1968 Memphis Speech

≡ ACTIVITIES

1. INTRODUCTION TO UNIT
Your teacher presents the purpose of the unit and explains the idea of making evidence-based claims.

2. INDEPENDENT READING
You independently read part of the text with a Guiding Question to help focus your reading.

3. READ ALOUD AND CLASS DISCUSSION
You follow along as you listen to the text being read aloud, and your teacher leads a discussion about it.

4. MODEL THE FORMING OF EBCs
Your teacher shows you how to form evidence-based claims about texts.

QUESTIONING PATH TOOL

Dr. King's Memphis Speech, Excerpt 1, Paragraphs 1–9

APPROACHING: *I determine my reading purposes and approach. I take note of key information about the text.*

I will initially focus on the author's *perspective* and the *structure* of the speech, then consider *language*, *ideas*, and supporting details. I will think about what the speaker's purpose might be in giving the speech.

QUESTIONING: *I use Guiding Questions to help me investigate the text.*

1. What do I learn about the author and the purpose for writing the text? [P]

2. What do I notice about how the text is organized or sequenced? [S]

ANALYZING: *I question further to connect and analyze the details I find (from the Guiding Questions Handout).*

3. How might I summarize the main ideas of the text and the key supporting details? [I]

4. How do specific words or phrases influence the meaning or tone of the text? [L]

DEEPENING: *I consider the questions of others.*

EXTENDING: *I pose my own questions.*

APPROACHING TEXTS TOOL

Name _____ Text _____

APPROACHING THE TEXT	
Before reading, I consider what my specific purposes for reading are.	**What are my reading purposes?**
I also take note of key information about the text.	**Title:** **Author:** **Source/Publisher:**
	Text type: **Publication date:**
	What do I already think or understand about the text based on this information?

QUESTIONING THE TEXT	
As I read the text for the first time, I use Guiding Questions that relate to my reading purpose and focus. (*Can be taken from the Guiding Questions Handout.*)	**Guiding Questions for *my first reading* of the text:**
	As I read I mark details on the text that relate to my Guiding Questions.
As I reread, I use questions I have about specific details that have emerged in my reading to focus my analysis and deepen my understanding.	**Text-specific questions to help focus *my rereading* of the text:**

ODELL
EDUCATION

QUESTIONING PATH TOOL

Dr. King's Memphis Speech, Excerpt 2, Paragraphs 10–20

APPROACHING:
I determine my reading purposes and take note of key information about the text. I identify the LIPS domain(s) that will guide my initial reading.

I will initially focus on the author's *perspective* and the *structure* of the speech, then consider *language, ideas,* and supporting details. I will think about what the speaker's purpose might be in giving the speech.

QUESTIONING: *I use Guiding Questions to help me investigate the text (from the **Guiding Questions Handout**).*

1. What do I learn about the author and the purpose for writing the text? [P]

2. What do I notice about how the text is organized or sequenced? [S]

ANALYZING: *I question further to connect and analyze the details I find (from the **Guiding Questions Handout**).*

3. How might I summarize the main ideas of the text and the key supporting details? [I]

4. How do specific words or phrases influence the meaning or tone of the text? [L]

DEEPENING: *I consider the questions of others.*

5. At the end of paragraph 9, Dr. King states, "I'm happy . . . to be in Memphis." In the paragraphs that follow this statement, he makes a simple claim about the reason he supports the Memphis sanitation workers' strike: "The issue is injustice," and then states that "we've got to march again." Why does he make this claim?

6. What experiences and stories from previous civil rights protests does Dr. King then connect to the Memphis workers' strike?

7. At the start of paragraph 18, Dr. King tells his audience: "Now the other thing we'll have to do is this: Always anchor our external direct action with the power of economic withdrawal." What do the phrases "external direct action" and "power of economic withdrawal" mean in this statement?

8. What evidence does Dr. King then provide to explain why there is potential "power" for the nonwhite poor of America in "withdrawing economic support" from businesses that do not stand up for "fair treatment"?

EXTENDING: *I pose my own questions.*

QUESTIONING PATH TOOL

Dr. King's Memphis Speech, Excerpt 3, Paragraphs 21–28

APPROACHING: *I determine my reading purposes and approach. I take note of key information about the text.*

I will initially focus on the author's *perspective* and the *structure* of the speech, then consider *language*, *ideas*, and supporting details. I will think about what the speaker's purpose might be in giving the speech.

QUESTIONING: *I use guiding questions to help me investigate the text.*

1. What do I learn about the author and the purpose for writing the text? [P]

2. What do I notice about how the text is organized or sequenced? [S]

ANALYZING: *I question further to connect and analyze the details I find.*

3. How might I summarize the main ideas of the text and the key supporting details? [I]

4. How do specific words or phrases influence the meaning or tone of the text? [L]

DEEPENING: *I consider others' text-specific questions.*

5. Why does Dr. King make these four related claims in paragraphs 21–22?

   - "…we've got to give ourselves to this struggle until the end."

   - "Nothing would be more tragic than to stop at this point in Memphis."

   - "We've got to see it through."

   - "…either we go up together, or we go down together."

6. At the start of paragraph 23, Dr. King tells his audience, "Let us develop a kind of dangerous unselfishness." How does he use the story of the Priest, the Levite, and the Good Samaritan to illustrate what he means by "dangerous unselfishness"?

7. What is the question he wants his listeners to have in their minds as they go forth in support of the Memphis sanitation workers? Why?

EXTENDING: *I pose my own text-specific questions.*

ODELL
EDUCATION

ANALYZING DETAILS TOOL

Name _____   Text _____

Reading purpose:

A question I have about the text:

SEARCHING FOR DETAILS

I read the text closely and mark words and phrases that help me think about my question.

SELECTING DETAILS

I select words or phrases from my search that I think are the most important in thinking about my question.

Detail 1 (Ref.:)	Detail 2 (Ref.:)	Detail 3 (Ref.:)

ANALYZING DETAILS

I reread parts of the text and think about the meaning of the details and what they tell me about my question.

What I think about detail 1:	What I think about detail 2:	What I think about detail 3:

CONNECTING DETAILS

I compare the details and explain the connections I see among them.

How I connect the details:

ODELL
EDUCATION

FORMING EVIDENCE-BASED CLAIMS TOOL

Name _ _ _ _ _ _ _ _ _ _ _ _ _ Text _ _ _ _ _ _ _ _ _ _ _ _ _

A question I have about the text:

FINDING DETAILS I find interesting details that are <u>related</u> and that stand out to me from reading the text closely.	Detail 1 (Ref.:)	Detail 2 (Ref.:)	Detail 3 (Ref.:)

CONNECTING THE DETAILS I reread and think about the details, and <u>explain</u> the connections I find among them.	What I think about detail 1:	What I think about detail 2:	What I think about detail 3:

How I connect the details:

MAKING A CLAIM I state a conclusion that I have come to and can support with <u>evidence</u> from the text after reading and thinking about it closely.	My claim about the text:

ODELL EDUCATION

SUPPORTING EVIDENCE-BASED CLAIMS TOOL

Name _____ **Text** _ _ _ _ _ _ _ _ _

CLAIM:

Supporting Evidence	Supporting Evidence	Supporting Evidence

(Reference:) (Reference:) (Reference:)

CLAIM:

Supporting Evidence	Supporting Evidence	Supporting Evidence

(Reference:) (Reference:) (Reference:)

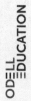

SUPPORTING EVIDENCE-BASED CLAIMS TOOL

Name

Text

CLAIM:

Supporting Evidence

Supporting Evidence

Supporting Evidence

(Reference:)   (Reference:)   (Reference:)

CLAIM:

Supporting Evidence

Supporting Evidence

Supporting Evidence

(Reference:)   (Reference:)   (Reference:)

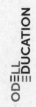

PART 2

MAKING EVIDENCE-BASED CLAIMS

Overview and Tools

"I've been to the mountaintop."

OBJECTIVE:	To develop the ability to make evidence-based claims through a close reading of a second text.

MATERIALS:
- *Supporting EBC Tool*
- *Attending to Details Handout*
- *Forming EBC Tool*
- *Questioning Path Tool*

TEXTS
- **1 Martin Luther King's 1968 Memphis Speech**

ACTIVITIES

1. INDEPENDENT READING TO FIND SUPPORTING EVIDENCE
You independently read part of the text and use the *Supporting EBC Tool* to look for evidence to support a claim made by the teacher.

2. READ ALOUD AND CLASS DISCUSSION
You follow along as you listen to the same part of the text being read aloud and then discuss it.

3. FINDING SUPPORTING EVIDENCE IN PAIRS
In pairs, you use the *Supporting EBC Tool* to look for evidence to support additional claims about the text made by the teacher.

4. CLASS DISCUSSION OF EBCs
The class discusses the evidence you have found to support the claims.

5. FORMING EBCs IN PAIRS
In pairs, you use the *Forming EBC Tool* to make an evidence-based claim of your own and present it to the class.

SUPPORTING EVIDENCE-BASED CLAIMS TOOL

Name - - - - - - - - - - - - - - - -

Text - - - - - - - - - - - - - - - -

CLAIM:

Supporting Evidence	Supporting Evidence	Supporting Evidence

(Reference: ____) (Reference: ____) (Reference: ____)

CLAIM:

Supporting Evidence	Supporting Evidence	Supporting Evidence

(Reference: ____) (Reference: ____) (Reference: ____)

QUESTIONING PATH TOOL

Dr. King's Memphis, Excerpt 4, Paragraphs 29–52 (end)

APPROACHING:
I determine my reading purposes and take note of key information about the text. I identify the LIPS domain(s) that will guide my initial reading.

I will initially focus on the author's *perspective* and the *structure* of the speech, then consider *language*, *ideas*, and supporting details. I will think about what the speaker's purpose might be in giving the speech.

QUESTIONING: *I use Guiding Questions to help me investigate the text (from the Guiding Questions Handout).*

1. What do I learn about the author and the purpose for writing the text? [P]

2. What do I notice about how the text is organized or sequenced? [S]

ANALYZING: *I question further to connect and analyze the details I find (from the Guiding Questions Handout).*

3. What claims do I find in the text? [I]

4. How do specific words or phrases influence the meaning or tone of the text? [L]

DEEPENING: *I consider the questions of others.*

5. In the final section of the speech, King tells a story from his own recent experience of being attacked and then receiving a letter of support from an unlikely source. What are the key details of this story, and why are they important?

6. In response to the story he tells, King says, "I want to say tonight that I too am happy that I didn't sneeze." What reasons does he present for making this claim, with each reason introduced with the repeated phrase "If I had sneezed . . ."?

7. Dr. King concludes his Memphis speech by saying, "Well, I don't know what will happen now. We've got some difficult days ahead. But it really doesn't matter with me now, because I've been to the mountaintop. And I don't mind."

   From what he says after these sentences, what do you think Dr. King meant?

   How does knowing what happened soon after Dr. King spoke these famous lines change how you think about and understand them?

EXTENDING: *I pose my own questions.*

SUPPORTING EVIDENCE-BASED CLAIMS TOOL

Name _ _ _ _ _ _ _ _ _ _ _ _ _ Text _ _ _ _ _ _ _ _ _ _ _ _ _

CLAIM:

Supporting Evidence	Supporting Evidence	Supporting Evidence
(Reference:)	(Reference:)	(Reference:)

CLAIM:

Supporting Evidence	Supporting Evidence	Supporting Evidence
(Reference:)	(Reference:)	(Reference:)

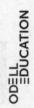

ODELL
EDUCATION

SUPPORTING EVIDENCE-BASED CLAIMS TOOL

Name _ **Text** _ _ _ _ _ _ _ _ _ _ _

CLAIM:

Supporting Evidence	Supporting Evidence	Supporting Evidence

(Reference:)   **(Reference:**)   **(Reference:**)

CLAIM:

Supporting Evidence	Supporting Evidence	Supporting Evidence

(Reference:)   **(Reference:**)   **(Reference:**)

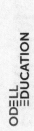

ODELL EDUCATION

FORMING EVIDENCE-BASED CLAIMS TOOL

Name _ Text _

A question I have about the text:

FINDING DETAILS	Detail 1 (Ref.:)	Detail 2 (Ref.:)	Detail 3 (Ref.:)
I find interesting details that are related and that stand out to me from reading the text closely.			

CONNECTING THE DETAILS	What I think about detail 1:	What I think about detail 2:	What I think about detail 3:
I reread and think about the details, and explain the connections I find among them.			

How I connect the details:

MAKING A CLAIM	My claim about the text:
I state a conclusion that I have come to and can support with evidence from the text after reading and thinking about it closely.	

ODELL
EDUCATION

PART 3

ORGANIZING EVIDENCE-BASED CLAIMS

Overview and Tools

"We organized!"

OBJECTIVE:	To learn to develop and explain evidence-based claims through the selection and organization of supporting evidence.

MATERIALS:
- *Organizing EBC Tool*
- *Forming EBC Tool*
- *Questioning Path Tool*

TEXTS:
- 2 Cesar Chavez's 1984 California Commonwealth Address

ACTIVITIES

1. INDEPENDENT READING AND FINDING EBCs
You independently read a second text and use the *Forming EBC Tool* to make an evidence-based claim.

2. COMPARING EBCs
You compare your claims with your peers. Then you read the text to look for more evidence to support your claim.

3. MODEL THE ORGANIZING OF EBCs
Your teacher models organizing evidence to develop and explain claims.

4. DEEPENING UNDERSTANDING
As a class, you use questions to deepen your understanding of the text and develop another evidence-based claim.

5. ORGANIZING EBCs IN PAIRS
In pairs, you develop and organize a new claim with using the *Organizing EBC Tool*.

6. CLASS DISCUSSION OF STUDENT EBCs
You discuss the evidence-based claims you have developed with the class.

QUESTIONING PATH TOOL
Cesar Chavez's Commonwealth Club Address

APPROACHING: *I determine my reading purposes and take note of key information about the text. I identify the LIPS domain(s) that will guide my initial reading.*

I will initially focus on the author's *perspective* and the *structure* of the speech, then consider *language*, *ideas*, and supporting details. I will think about what the speaker's purpose might be in giving the speech.

QUESTIONING: *I use Guiding Questions to help me investigate the text (from the **Guiding Questions Handout**).*

1. What do I learn about the author and the purpose for writing the text? [P]
2. What do I think the text is mainly about—what is discussed in detail? [I]

ANALYZING: *I question further to connect and analyze the details I find (from the **Guiding Questions Handout**).*

3. How might I summarize the main ideas of the text and the key supporting details? [I]
4. How do specific words or phrases influence the meaning or tone of the text? [L]

DEEPENING: *I consider the questions of others.*

5. What are the key details of the story Chavez tells to begin his speech?

   Why is this story—and what Chavez says about the living conditions of farm workers in paragraphs 5–10—important to understanding what he says at the start of paragraph 11?

6. Chavez declares, "All my life, I have been driven by one dream, one goal, one vision." What is that dream—and why does he have it?

   How has Chavez's "one dream" grown from the details of his life and his "own experience with racism"?

7. What does Chavez tell his audience was the way he and others "attacked that historical source of shame and infamy that our people in this country lived with . . . attacked that injustice"?

   What does his speech claim about the importance of "organizing" and the UFW?

8. Chavez makes two related claims about the importance of the UFW to all Hispanics:

   "All Hispanics—urban and rural, young and old—are connected to the farm workers' experience. We had all lived through the fields—or our parents had. We shared that common humiliation."

   "And Hispanics across California and the nation who don't work in agriculture are better off today because of what the farm workers taught people about organization, about pride and strength, about seizing control over their own lives."

   What arguments and evidence does Chavez present to support these claims?

9. What "two major trends [that] give us hope and encouragement" does Chavez mention? How might these trends lead to a day "when we win the economic and political rewards which are in keeping with our numbers in society"?

10. Chavez ends his speech by quoting from the New Testament: "That the last shall be first and the first shall be last." How does this quotation relate to the ideas and historical details about the UFW and Hispanics in the United States that he has presented throughout his speech?

EXTENDING: *I pose my own questions.*

ODELL
EDUCATION

FORMING EVIDENCE-BASED CLAIMS TOOL

Name _____ **Text** _____

A question I have about the text:

FINDING DETAILS

I find interesting details that are related and that stand out to me from reading the text closely.

Detail 1 (Ref.:   )

Detail 2 (Ref.:   )

Detail 3 (Ref.:   )

CONNECTING THE DETAILS

I reread and think about the details, and explain the connections I find among them.

What I think about detail 1:

What I think about detail 2:

What I think about detail 3:

How I connect the details:

MAKING A CLAIM

I state a conclusion that I have come to and can support with evidence from the text after reading and thinking about it closely.

My claim about the text:

ODELL EDUCATION

ORGANIZING EVIDENCE-BASED CLAIMS TOOL (2 POINTS)

Name _ _ _ _ _ _ _ _ _ _ _ _   Text _ _ _ _ _ _ _ _ _ _ _ _ _

CLAIM:

Point 1

A Supporting Evidence	B Supporting Evidence
(Reference:)	(Reference:)

C Supporting Evidence	D Supporting Evidence
(Reference:)	(Reference:)

Point 2

A Supporting Evidence	B Supporting Evidence
(Reference:)	(Reference:)

C Supporting Evidence	D Supporting Evidence
(Reference:)	(Reference:)

ODELL EDUCATION

ORGANIZING EVIDENCE-BASED CLAIMS TOOL (3 POINTS)

Name _ _ _ _ _ _ _ _ _ _ _ _ Text _ _ _ _ _ _ _ _ _ _ _ _

CLAIM:

Point 1

	Supporting Evidence	
A		
(Reference:		)
B	Supporting Evidence	
(Reference:		)
C	Supporting Evidence	
(Reference:		)

Point 2

	Supporting Evidence	
A		
(Reference:		)
B	Supporting Evidence	
(Reference:		)
C	Supporting Evidence	
(Reference:		)

Point 3

	Supporting Evidence	
A		
(Reference:		)
B	Supporting Evidence	
(Reference:		)
C	Supporting Evidence	
(Reference:		)

FORMING EVIDENCE-BASED CLAIMS TOOL

Name _____   Text _____

A question I have about the text:

FINDING DETAILS

I find interesting details that are _related_ and that stand out to me from reading the text closely.

Detail 1 (Ref.:)	Detail 2 (Ref.:)	Detail 3 (Ref.:)

CONNECTING THE DETAILS

I reread and think about the details, and _explain_ the connections I find among them.

What I think about detail 1:	What I think about detail 2:	What I think about detail 3:

How I connect the details:

MAKING A CLAIM

I state a conclusion that I have come to and can support with _evidence_ from the text after reading and thinking about it closely.

My claim about the text:

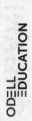

ORGANIZING EVIDENCE-BASED CLAIMS TOOL (2 POINTS)

Name _ _ _ _ _ _ _ _ _ _ _ _ _ Text _ _ _ _ _ _ _ _ _ _

CLAIM:

Point 1

A Supporting Evidence	B Supporting Evidence
(Reference:)	(Reference:)
C Supporting Evidence	D Supporting Evidence
(Reference:)	(Reference:)

Point 2

A Supporting Evidence	B Supporting Evidence
(Reference:)	(Reference:)
C Supporting Evidence	D Supporting Evidence
(Reference:)	(Reference:)

ORGANIZING EVIDENCE-BASED CLAIMS TOOL (3 POINTS)

Name _ _ _ _ _ _ _ _ _ _ _ _ _ _ _ Text _ _ _ _ _ _ _ _ _ _ _ _ _ _ _

CLAIM:

Point 1

A   Supporting Evidence

(Reference:)

B   Supporting Evidence

(Reference:)

C   Supporting Evidence

(Reference:)

Point 2

A   Supporting Evidence

(Reference:)

B   Supporting Evidence

(Reference:)

C   Supporting Evidence

(Reference:)

Point 3

A   Supporting Evidence

(Reference:)

B   Supporting Evidence

(Reference:)

C   Supporting Evidence

(Reference:)

ODELL EDUCATION

FORMING EVIDENCE-BASED CLAIMS TOOL

Name _ _ _ _ _ _ _ _ _ _ _ _ _ _ **Text** _ _ _ _ _ _ _ _ _ _ _ _ _ _

A question I have about the text:

FINDING DETAILS	**Detail 1 (Ref.:**)	**Detail 2 (Ref.:**)	**Detail 3 (Ref.:**)
I find interesting details that are related and that stand out to me from reading the text closely.			

CONNECTING THE DETAILS	**What I think about detail 1:**	**What I think about detail 2:**	**What I think about detail 3:**
I reread and think about the details, and explain the connections I find among them.			

How I connect the details:

MAKING A CLAIM	**My claim about the text:**
I state a conclusion that I have come to and can support with evidence from the text after reading and thinking about it closely.	

ODELL EDUCATION

PART 4

WRITING EBCs

Overview and Tools

"And on that day, our nation shall fulfill its creed"

OBJECTIVE:	To develop the ability to express text-based claims through writing.

MATERIALS:
- *Writing EBC Handout*
- *Questioning Path Tool*
- *Forming EBC Tool*
- *Organizing EBC Tool*

TEXT:
- 3 Janet Murguia's "A Single Garment of Destiny" 2008 Speech

ACTIVITIES

1. MODEL THE COMMUNICATION OF AN EBC THROUGH WRITING
Your teacher shows you how to write paragraphs that express an evidence-based claim.

2. MODEL AND PRACTICE THE USE OF QUESTIONS AND CRITERIA TO IMPROVE A WRITTEN EBC
Your teacher introduces a process for improving writing with your classmates.

3. WRITING EBCs IN PAIRS
In pairs, you develop a paragraph that expresses an evidence-based claim.

4. REVIEWING AND IMPROVING WRITTEN EBCs
You and your partner present your written evidence-based claims to your other classmates for feedback.

5. INDEPENDENT READING, DEVELOPING QUESTIONING PATHS, AND MAKING EBCs
You read and question another text with a *Questioning Path Tool* and use the *Forming EBC Tool* to develop another evidence-based claim.

6. READ ALOUD AND CLASS DISCUSSION
You discuss your new evidence-based with the class.

7. INDEPENDENT WRITING OF EBCs
You organize your claim with an *Organizing EBC Tool* for the claim and draft a one- to two-paragraph evidence-based claim.

8. USING PEER FEEDBACK TO REVISE A WRITTEN EBCs
You review your claim with a partner.

ODELL
EDUCATION

QUESTIONING PATH TOOL

Name: _____   **Text:** _____

APPROACHING: *I determine my reading purposes and take note of key information about the text. I identify the LIPS domain(s) that will guide my initial reading.*	Purpose: Key information: LIPS domain(s):
QUESTIONING: *I use Guiding Questions to help me investigate the text (from the **Guiding Questions Handout**).*	1. 2.
ANALYZING: *I question further to connect and analyze the details I find (from the **Guiding Questions Handout**).*	1. 2.
DEEPENING: *I consider the questions of others.*	1. 2. 3.
EXTENDING: *I pose my own questions.*	1. 2.

FORMING EVIDENCE-BASED CLAIMS TOOL

Name _ _ _ _ _ _ _ _ _ _ _ _ _ _ Text _

A question I have about the text:

FINDING DETAILS I find interesting details that are related and that stand out to me from reading the text closely.	**Detail 1 (Ref.:)**	**Detail 2 (Ref.:)**	**Detail 3 (Ref.:)**

CONNECTING THE DETAILS I reread and think about the details, and explain the connections I find among them.	**What I think about detail 1:**	**What I think about detail 2:**	**What I think about detail 3:**
	How I connect the details:		

MAKING A CLAIM I state a conclusion that I have come to and can support with evidence from the text after reading and thinking about it closely.	**My claim about the text:**

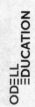
ODELL
EDUCATION

ORGANIZING EVIDENCE-BASED CLAIMS TOOL (2 POINTS)

Name _ _ _ _ _ _ _ _ _ _ _ _ _ _ _ _ _ Text _ _ _ _ _ _ _ _ _ _ _ _ _ _ _ _ _

CLAIM:

Point 1

A Supporting Evidence	B Supporting Evidence
(Reference:)	(Reference:)

C Supporting Evidence	D Supporting Evidence
(Reference:)	(Reference:)

Point 2

A Supporting Evidence	B Supporting Evidence
(Reference:)	(Reference:)

C Supporting Evidence	D Supporting Evidence
(Reference:)	(Reference:)

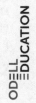

ODELL EDUCATION

ORGANIZING EVIDENCE-BASED CLAIMS TOOL (3 POINTS)

Name _ _ _ _ _ _ _ _ _ _ Text _ _ _ _ _ _ _ _ _ _

CLAIM:

Point 1

A	Supporting Evidence

(Reference:)

B	Supporting Evidence

(Reference:)

C	Supporting Evidence

(Reference:)

Point 2

A	Supporting Evidence

(Reference:)

B	Supporting Evidence

(Reference:)

C	Supporting Evidence

(Reference:)

Point 3

A	Supporting Evidence

(Reference:)

B	Supporting Evidence

(Reference:)

C	Supporting Evidence

(Reference:)

PART 5

DEVELOPING EVIDENCE-BASED WRITING

Overview and Tools

"A single garment of destiny"

OBJECTIVE:	To develop the ability to express global evidence-based claims in writing.

MATERIALS:
- *Forming EBC Tool*
- *Organizing EBC Tool*
- *Writing EBC Handout*
- *Making EBC Literacy Skills Rubric*
- *Student Making EBC Literacy Skills Checklist*
- *Student Making EBC Academic Habits Checklist*

TEXT:
- 1 **Martin Luther King's 1968 Memphis Speech**
- 2 **Cesar Chavez's 1984 California Commonwealth Address**
- 3 **Janet Murguia's "A Single Garment of Destiny" 2008 Speech**

ACTIVITIES

1. INDEPENDENT READING AND CLASS DISCUSSION OF GLOBAL EBCs
You review all texts you have read in the unit, and the class discusses global and comparative evidence-based claims.

2. FORMING GLOBAL OR COMPARATIVE EBCs
You review previous claims and use a *Forming EBC Tool* to frame a new, comparative, or global evidence-based claim.

3. REVIEWING AND ORGANIZING EBCs
You discuss your new claims in pairs and then with the class, thinking about how you will organize it with an *Organizing EBC Tool*.

4. INDEPENDENT DRAFTING OF A FINAL WRITTEN EBC ESSAY
You draft a final evidence-based claims essay using your new claims.

5. USING THE COLLABORATIVE, CRITERIA-BASED PROCESS TO IMPROVE ESSAYS
You use a criteria-based checklist and feedback from peers to revise and improve your evidence-based claims essays.

6. CLASS DISCUSSION OF FINAL EBC ESSAYS
You discuss your final EBC essays and reflect on the literacy skills and academic habits involved in making and communicating evidence-based claims.

FORMING EVIDENCE-BASED CLAIMS TOOL

Name _ _ _ _ _ _ _ _ _ _ _ _ _ _ _ _ _ _   Text _ _ _ _ _ _ _ _ _ _ _ _ _ _ _ _

A question I have about the text:

FINDING DETAILS I find interesting details that are <u>related</u> and that stand out to me from reading the text closely.	Detail 1 (Ref.:)	Detail 2 (Ref.:)	Detail 3 (Ref.:

CONNECTING THE DETAILS I reread and think about the details, and explain the connections I find among them.	What I think about detail 1:	What I think about detail 2:	What I think about detail 3:

	How I connect the details:

MAKING A CLAIM I state a conclusion that I have come to and can support with evidence from the text after reading and thinking about it closely.	My claim about the text:

ODELL EDUCATION

SUPPORTING EVIDENCE-BASED CLAIMS TOOL

Name _ _ _ _ _ _ _ _ _ _ _ _ _ _   Text _ _ _ _ _ _ _ _ _ _ _ _ _ _

CLAIM:

Supporting Evidence	Supporting Evidence	Supporting Evidence

(Reference:)   (Reference:)   (Reference:)

CLAIM:

Supporting Evidence	Supporting Evidence	Supporting Evidence

(Reference:)   (Reference:)   (Reference:)

ORGANIZING EVIDENCE-BASED CLAIMS TOOL (2 POINTS)

Name _ _ _ _ _ _ _ _ _ _ _ Text _ _ _ _ _ _ _ _ _ _ _

CLAIM:

Point 1

A Supporting Evidence	B Supporting Evidence
(Reference:)	(Reference:)
C Supporting Evidence	D Supporting Evidence
(Reference:)	(Reference:)

Point 2

A Supporting Evidence	B Supporting Evidence
(Reference:)	(Reference:)
C Supporting Evidence	D Supporting Evidence
(Reference:)	(Reference:)

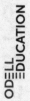

ODELL
EDUCATION

ORGANIZING EVIDENCE-BASED CLAIMS TOOL (3 POINTS)

Name _ _ _ _ _ _ _ _ _ _ _ _ _ _ Text _ _ _ _ _ _ _ _ _ _ _ _ _

CLAIM:

Point 1

A	Supporting Evidence

(Reference:)

B	Supporting Evidence

(Reference:)

C	Supporting Evidence

(Reference:)

Point 2

A	Supporting Evidence

(Reference:)

B	Supporting Evidence

(Reference:)

C	Supporting Evidence

(Reference:)

Point 3

A	Supporting Evidence

(Reference:)

B	Supporting Evidence

(Reference:)

C	Supporting Evidence

(Reference:)

ODELL
EDUCATION

STUDENT MAKING EVIDENCE-BASED CLAIMS ACADEMIC HABITS CHECKLIST

Academic Habits Used in This Unit	✔	EVIDENCE Demonstrating the HABITS
1. **Engaging Actively:** Focuses attention on the task when working individually and with others		
2. **Collaborating:** Works respectfully and productively to help a group be successful		
3. **Communicating Clearly:** Presents ideas and supporting evidence so others can understand them		
4. **Listening:** Pays attention to ideas from others and takes time to think about them		
5. **Understanding Purpose and Process:** Understands why and how a task should be accomplished		
6. **Revising:** Rethinks ideas and refines work based on feedback from others		
7. **Remaining Open:** Modifies and further justifies ideas in response to thinking from others		
Comments:		

ODELL EDUCATION

STUDENT MAKING EVIDENCE-BASED CLAIMS LITERACY SKILLS CHECKLIST

LITERACY SKILLS USED IN THIS UNIT	✔	EVIDENCE Demonstrating the SKILLS
READING		
1. **Attending to Details:** Identifies words, details, or quotations that are important to understanding the text		
2. **Interpreting Language:** Understands how words are used to express ideas and perspectives		
3. **Identifying Relationships:** Notices important connections among details, ideas, or texts		
4. **Recognizing Perspective:** Identifies and explains the author's view of the text's topic		
THINKING		
5. **Making Inferences:** Draws sound conclusions from reading and examining the text closely		
6. **Forming Claims:** States a meaningful conclusion that is well-supported by evidence from the text		
7. **Using Evidence:** Uses well-chosen details from the text to explain and support claims; accurately paraphrases or quotes		
WRITING		
8. **Presenting Details:** Inserts details and quotations effectively into written or spoken explanations		
9. **Organizing Ideas:** Organizes claims, supporting ideas, and evidence in a logical order		
10. **Using Language:** Writes and speaks clearly so others can understand claims and ideas		
11. **Using Conventions:** Correctly uses sentence elements, punctuation, and spelling to produce clear writing		
12. **Publishing:** Correctly uses, formats, and cites textual evidence to support claims		
General comments:		

UNIT 3

RESEARCHING TO DEEPEN
UNDERSTANDING

DEVELOPING CORE LITERACY
PROFICIENCIES

GRADE 7

Water: Why is it so valuable?

ODELL
EDUCATION

GOAL

In this unit you will develop your proficiency as an investigator and user of information. You will learn how to do the following:

1. Have an inquiring mind and ask good questions.
2. Search for information—in texts, interviews, and on the Internet—that can help you answer your questions.
3. Record and organize the information you find.
4. Decide what is relevant and trustworthy in the sources of your information.
5. Come to a research-based perspective on a topic.
6. Clearly communicate what you have learned and "tell the story" of how you've come to learn it.

TOPIC

In this unit, you will explore the one of our most fundamental needs: water. You will learn about the importance and abundance of water on our planet and then go deeper into the topic by reading about how management of water is vital to human survival and the ecosystems they live in.

ACTIVITIES

Throughout the unit, you will watch videos, read texts, and discuss the many aspects of water with your class. As you explore the topic, you will determine what you want to explore through research. As you read sources closely, you will keep an organized portfolio. Using your notes, you will express your new knowledge in a reflective research narrative.

TERMS AND DEFINITIONS USED IN THIS UNIT

Topic

the general topic chosen for class exploration

Area of investigation

A particular theme, question, problem, or more focused subtopic within the general topic that warrants investigation

Inquiry Questions

Questions posed by researchers about their Areas of Investigation to be answered through inquiry

Inquiry Path

A realm of inquiry stemming from one or more related Inquiry Questions; a path can be framed by a general question that summarizes more specific questions or subtopics

Research frame

An organized set of Inquiry Questions or Paths that guide the research process

Research portfolio

The binder or electronic folder where you physically or electronically store and organize all the material related to your personal research

Research plan

An organizer presenting the process you follow to guide you through the various stages of inquiry

RESEARCHING TO DEEPEN UNDERSTANDING LITERACY TOOLBOX

In *Researching to Deepen Understanding*, you will begin to build your Literacy Toolbox by learning how to use the following handouts, tools, and checklists organized in your Student Edition.

 HANDOUTS

To support your work with the texts and the tools, you will be able to use the following informational handouts. You will also use handouts from previous Core Proficiencies units:

Research Plan

This handout presents the process you will follow during the various stages of inquiry.

Research Portfolio

This handout will help you to organize your tools and analysis throughout the research process.

Attending to Details Handout

from the *Reading Closely* unit

Guiding Questions Handout

from the *Reading Closely* unit

Posing Inquiry Questions Handout

This handout helps you come up with good questions to ask about a topic. These questions help you find out important information throughout your research.

Assessing Sources Handout

This handout helps you evaluate how useful a potential source will be for your research.

Connecting Ideas Handout

This handout gives you examples of words to use in making connections among ideas in your writing.

Researching to Deepen Understanding—Final Writing Task Handout

This handout explains to you what you will be doing in the final assignment for this unit: writing a reflective research narrative that tells the story of how you arrived at your research-based perspective on the topic and communicates your experience with the inquiry process. The handout will also help you know what your teacher will be looking for so you can be successful writing your narrative.

 **TOOLS**

In addition to using the handouts, you will learn how to use the following tools. You will also use tools from previous Developing Core Literacy Proficiencies units:

Forming Evidence-Based Claims Research Tool

from the *Making Evidence-Based Claims* unit (with Inquiry Question)

Organizing Evidence-Based Claims Research Tool

from the *Making Evidence-Based Claims* unit (with Inquiry Path)

Exploring a Topic Tool

This tool helps you think about potential areas of the topic you want to explore through research.

Potential Sources Tool

This tool helps you collect and organize information on sources you find that might be useful in your research.

Taking Notes Tool

This tool helps you make and organize notes from the various sources you find throughout your research.

Research Frame Tool

This tool helps you determine what you need to explore in order to develop a deep understanding of your area of investigation.

Research Evaluation Tool

This tool helps you work with your peers and teacher to determine if you have found enough information about your area of investigation.

CHECKLISTS

You will also use these checklists throughout the unit to support peer- and self-review:

Researching to Deepen Understanding Skills and Habits Checklist

This checklist presents and briefly describes the literacy skills and habits you will be working on during the unit. You can use it to remind you of what you are trying to learn. You can also use it to reflect on what you have done when reading, discussing, or writing. It can help you give feedback to other students about their research. Your teacher may use it to let you know about your areas of strength and areas in which you need to improve.

Area Evaluation and Research Evaluation Checklists

These checklists help you keep track of the different activities you need to do while researching the topic. They also can help you think about how clearly you are able to express your topic and questions.

RESEARCHING TO DEEPEN
UNDERSTANDING COMMON
SOURCE SET

WATER: WHY IS IT SO VALUABLE?

<table>
<tr><td>NOTE</td></tr>
<tr><td>The unit uses texts that are accessible for free on the Internet without any login information, membership requirements, or purchase. Because of the ever-changing nature of website addresses, specific links are not provided. Teachers and students can locate these texts through web searches using the information provided.</td></tr>
</table>

Source 1: The first Common Source introduces a broad topic area in which to conduct research. It should be a high-interest source, preferably a video or multimedia resource. This source is used to stimulate curiosity and thinking about the topic and opens up many possibilities for research questions and learning within the topic area. This source is introduced and used in Part 1, Activity 2.

Common Source: "Introduction to Water"—Frank Gregorio, October 16, 2009. This Internet-based video can be found on YouTube.

Overview: This 3:47-minute video contains dramatic images of various forms of water and interesting facts about water. The video serves as an open introduction to the topic of water that can goad students to explore a number of different aspects of water whether its water's unique chemical attributes, life-sustaining value, or natural beauty.

Discussion Questions: What does the video suggest about the topic area, "Water: Why is it so valuable?" What other topics about water does it make you think about?

Source 2: The second Common Source provides background information and is used to extend discussion about the topic area. It also provides an opportunity to work on close-reading skills used during an independent research project. It is a print source that presents new information but is fairly easy to read and understand, and may be an Internet-based text. The source should expand thinking about the topic and open up additional paths for asking questions and learning within the topic area. All students read this source. This source is introduced and used in Part 1, Activity 2.

Common Source 2A: "Water-Introductory Text"—Zachary Odell, 2013. This article was written for the unit and is available following the Common Source Set.

Overview: The source is an article written by Zachary Odell for this unit and serves as another broad introduction to water. Reading this source opens up discussion about how water is an interesting molecule, affects the lives of animals and humans on earth, and is needed and used by humans for various reasons.

Alternative Common Source 2B: "How much water is on Earth"—Brett Israel, September 9, 2010. This article can be found on the livescience.com website.

Overview: This article begins with an intriguing graphic of the earth and two blue balls next to it that represent the planet's ocean water and freshwater. The article quotes David Gallo from the Woods Hole Oceanographic Institution to explain just how precious and rare water is. Israel also introduces some interesting facts about water including how less than 1 percent of the earth's freshwater is accessible and that six countries have 50 percent of freshwater reserves.

Discussion Questions: What does the video suggest about the topic area: "Water: Why is it so valuable?" What other topics about water does it make you think about?

Source 3: The third Common Source is a set of resources that introduce various subtopics within the general topic area. These sources provide additional background information and thinking to help make decisions about a more focused direction for research. The texts in this Source Set are also used to practice the skills of assessing sources for their relationship to research questions, their accessibility and interest, and their credibility and relevance within the topic area. Students read *one* of these sources, depending on their interests. This source is introduced and used in Part 1, Activity 3.

Common Sources

Source 3A—Water in the Solar System: "The Solar System and Beyond Is Awash in Water"—National Aeronautics and Space Administration (NASA). This source can be found on the NASA website, www.nasa.gov.

Source 3B—Water-Stressed Countries: "Why Water"—Blue Planet Network. This source can be found on the Blue Planet Network's website, www.blueplanetnetwork.org.

Source 3C—Sustainable Use of Water: "Water Footprint of an American"—The Nature Conservancy, 2011. This source can be found on The Nature Conservancy website, www.nature.org.

Overview: These three sources each focus the topic of water in a different direction and open up possible subtopic areas for research.

3A: This website opens up the possibilities of researching water in space. Although complex, mostly because of the specialized vocabulary of planets and moons, the NASA article gives good background information on how water is everywhere in the solar system. Located on the same web page is a visual graphic of "Ocean Worlds," which describes the many different bodies of water that have been found on moons of other planets and possibly Pluto as well.

3B: The Blue Planet Network website helps students discover why clean water is crucial for survival and uncovers the stunning number of people worldwide who do not have access to clean water. Students could begin by watching the embedded video. Students interested in this topic may choose to investigate the several links included on Blue Planet Network's website, such as "Stories about Water" or "Project Showcases."

3C: The "Water Footprint of an American" is an information graphic that explains exactly how much water the average American uses in one day, including water that is "hidden" and used to grow and make the food we eat, clothes we wear, and produce the energy we consume. This source also provides numerous links to other pages that provide additional information on how to use water responsibly, tracking down your own water usage and footprint, and ways that you can get involved in protecting our world's water.

Discussion Questions: What does the text suggest about the topic area: "Water: Why is it so valuable?" What questions or directions for research does it suggest to you?

Text Assessment Questions: How accessible and interesting is the text for you? How credible and relevant is the source as a starting point for further research?

Source 4: The fourth Common Source Set provides information about websites (or other resources) that can be used to start a search for new sources and information in one of several possible subtopic areas. Students investigate *one* of these websites, depending on their interests. This source is introduced and used in Part 1, Activity 3.

Common Sources and Overviews

Source 4A: Water in the Solar System: "Curiosity shows there's a lot more to Mars than thought"— Newsela, October 8, 2013. This news article, originally from the *Los Angeles Times,* describes how NASA's rover, *Curiosity,* has discovered traces of water on Mars. These discoveries lead scientists to think differently about the "red planet."

Source 4B: Water-Stressed Countries Issues: "Protecting Clean Water for People and Nature"—The Nature Conservancy web page. This web page includes several ways this organization approaches issues about water. You might use some of these to refine your research or explore other related topics.

Source 4C: Water Management Issues: "Is There Really a Water Crisis"—Maggie Koerth Baker, found on boingboing.net. This source is an interview with Asit Biswas, president of the Third World Centre for Water Management, who argues that there is no water shortage crisis but a crisis over the management of the existing water. It opens an interesting subtopic around water management and technologies associated with getting water to people and reusing wastewater.

Discussion Questions: What does the website suggest about the topic area: "Water: Why is it so valuable?" What questions or directions for research does it suggest to you?

Text Assessment Questions: How accessible and interesting is the website's text for you? How credible and relevant is the source as a starting point for further research?

Source 5: The fifth Common Source is a set of texts that present a range of perspectives on a subtopic within the overall topic area. These texts are ones that have been written for various purposes by a range of organizations or authors who view the topic area in somewhat different ways. This Source Set is used to practice the skills of reading to understand a text's perspective on a topic and to compare perspectives and the ways they are presented by different authors. Students read *one* of these sources as a class and *another* individually. This source is introduced and used in Part 3, Activity 2.

Common Sources

Source 5A: "A dwindling river: As water demands rise, the Colorado River is running dry."—Judith Cohen. This source can be found using the Gale Virtual Reference Library.

Source 5B: "The Unfiltered Truth about Water"—Evergreen AES. This source is from the Evergreen AES website, www.evergreenaes.com.

Source 5C: "The Coming Water Wars"—Princeton University. This source was published by Princeton University using the United Nations, *Montreal Gazette,* UNESCO, the *New York Times,* and Inter Press Service as sources.

Source 5D: "A dire shortage of water"—Emily Sohn, August 6, 2004. This source is available through the student.societyforscience.org website.

Overview: These four sources all present specific and differing perspectives on the subtopic area of water. They can be used to further understanding in the subtopic area and also to practice the skills of determining a source's perspective and therefore also its bias, credibility, and relevance to research in the topic area.

5A: This text details the ways in which the Colorado River is being depleted of water every day. The author's description of the geographic location of the Colorado River being near the southwest desert helps readers explore why this river is being threatened. The pictures and charts help summarize key pieces of information.

5B: "The Unfiltered Truth about Water" is an infographic that presents issues about water usage in the United States and offers possible solutions. Along with its images are pop-up bits of information that offer statistics and facts about water usage. The short, easy-to-read text has a clear and biased view of the issue and is an interesting text to discuss in terms of its credibility as well as its purpose and perspective.

5C: "The Coming Water Wars" is another infographic that probes the subtopic of water and war. The graphic presents information on the history of water issues, ratios between water availability and population, and how many people die because of the lack of clean water.

5D: "A dire shortage of water" is an article about a drought in the southwest United States and how droughts and water shortages are caused. Although this article is from 2004, its explanations are still applicable to current water issues.

Evaluating Perspective Questions

- What do I learn about the author and the purpose for writing the text? (GQH)
- What are the author's qualifications or credentials relative to the topic area? (ASH)
- What is the author's personal relationship to the topic area? (ASH)
- What details or words suggest the author's perspective? (GQH)
- How does the author's perspective influence the text's presentation of ideas or arguments? (GQH)
- How does the author's perspective and presentation of the text compare to others? (GQH)
- How does the author's perspective influence my reading of the text—and my use of the text in research? (GQH)

> **NOTE**
>
> Questions are referenced to handouts from the toolbox: GQH is the *Guiding Questions Handout* and ASH is the *Assessing Sources Handout*.

≡ ADDITIONAL RESOURCES IN THE TOPIC AREA

The following resources can be used to extend research. Some of these resources include additional webpages from the unit texts. Students can use these websites to pursue additional information related to water or deepen their understanding of the unit texts.

- "Water Facts"—Hound Studio (General Electric commercial), June 14, 2011
- "A country with no water"—TED Talk, Fahad Al-Attiya, April 2012
- "How to make filthy water drinkable"—TED Talk, Michael Pritchard, July 2009
- "Underground ocean on Jupiter's largest moon"—Earthsky.org, March 15, 2015

COMMON SOURCE 2A: WATER—INTRODUCTORY TEXT

Water is everywhere. We most often see it in oceans, lakes, rivers, and precipitation (e.g., rain and snow). It can also be found in deserts, underground, in the air, and in our bodies. Scientists have even found it in space. What is water? Water is a molecule or combination of the elements hydrogen and oxygen. The chemical formula for water is H_2O. People come into contact with many water molecules stuck together in one of three states: solid (ice), liquid (a pond), and gas (steam from a shower).

Maybe the most incredible thing about water is that there is always the same amount of water, just in different forms and in different places. Water moves around the Earth and atmosphere using the water cycle. Water is always changing states between ice, liquid, and gas.

As water moves through the water cycle and between its different states, it takes up space and interacts with both the living and nonliving world. It creates clouds and falls from the sky. It moves in the ocean making waves that splash on sand and rocks. It flows in underground rivers and rests in dark caverns beneath our feet. It floods fields of rice. And perhaps most importantly, it fills cells in plants and animals allowing us to live and breathe.

The movement and interaction of water with the nonliving world creates big holes in the Earth like the Grand Canyon, makes the rough edges of a pebble smooth, and produces large storms. Imagine you are a water molecule in snow on the top of a mountain. The sun's rays melt the bonds between you and your molecular friends and everyone changes state from a solid to a liquid. You begin to flow down the mountain in a cold stream. As you flow you move through and around rocks and other obstacles creating channels, waterfalls, and sharp turns. You join other water molecules from other streams getting bigger and wider. Now you have enough energy to make gullies and to move stones or as you flow around them, creating bends and riverbanks. You are now with billions of other molecules in a massive river, slowing down and spreading out on flat plains and emptying into an ocean. From the mountain to the valley you have broken and moved rocks, carved the land, and have interacted with living things along the way.

The flow, drip, collection and absorption of water on and into the land acts as a stage for life as it begins with and is sustained by H_2O. For the living world, water is the basic building block of life. Think of a pond, full of plants and animals. How did the pond get there? A depression or hole was created in the ground by flowing water. Water filled up the hole and begins to soak the nearby dirt. Plants begin to grow in the water and around the pond in wet spots (wetlands). The plants continue to grow as long as water is around. Animals, like fish or frogs that depend on the plants for food, make their home. Other animals that eat the birds and frogs, like raccoons or birds, are attracted to this place. A food web is created all because water shaped the ground and created the right place for this life to begin. The pond and the life that it supports together are called an ecosystem (the interaction between living and nonliving). On a sunny weekend morning a family comes to the pond to have a picnic and fish. It is their favorite spot. Water is important to this family in other ways as well.

People use water in many ways. Turn the handle on the tap in your kitchen or bathroom and water flows freely. It wasn't always so easy. Our ancestors around the world made the first homes near water because they knew their greatest chance for survival came with the life that water supported. It supported their lives. First they hunted and gathered animals and plants, but as they became more settled and created larger families, learned more about plants, and responded to changes in weather they began to farm. Growing plants requires water. This need for water began our long tradition of shaping the earth, creating machines, and making decisions all based on getting, moving, and using water.

Just like our ancestors we live near water, move water based upon our needs, and react to water as weather patterns change. These actions have serious impacts on us, our neighbors, our country and the world. There are more people now than ever before, which means there is more demand and dependency on water. Not just for drinking, but also for other things like recreation (e.g., fishing, boating, and vacation), transporting goods and materials (the Mississippi River), and agriculture (irrigation). Water also has spiritual and cultural meaning to us. There are places near water that define what home means for a community. Water is used in religious rituals, carrying important meaning for salvation and the afterlife.

Regardless of who we are or where we are from, we are connected to water. Our relationship with water and decisions about water are too important to ignore. Informed decisions result in sustainable use of water, like the Great Lakes Compact—an agreement between the states and Canadian provinces that surround the Great Lakes intended to ensure sustainable and collective decisions about how we use the water in these lakes. Selfish and uninformed decisions result in catastrophe such as the overuse of water in the Colorado River—it now runs dry 50 miles north of the Gulf of California. Whether we depend on water for drinking, washing, creating power, transporting, religious significance, food, or just to sit and watch we are all connected to water. However, it is important to remember that we need water. Water does not need us. We are responsible for being sustainable stewards of this resource.

RESEARCHING TO DEEPEN UNDERSTANDING

DEVELOPING CORE LITERACY PROFICIENCIES

GRADE 7

Literacy Toolbox

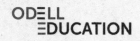

STUDENT RESEARCH PLAN

STUDENT RESEARCH PLAN		TOOLS AND HANDOUTS
I. INITIATING INQUIRY *I determine what I want to know about a topic and develop Inquiry Questions that I will investigate.*	**1. Exploring a Topic**	Exploring a Topic Potential Sources Area Evaluation Checklist Posing Inquiry Questions Handout
	2. Choosing an Area of Investigation	
	3. Generating Inquiry Questions	
II. GATHERING INFORMATION *I find and take notes on sources that will help me answer my Inquiry Questions and define the scope of my investigation.*	**1. Finding and Assessing Sources**	Potential Sources Assessing Sources Handout Taking Notes Research Frame Posing Inquiry Questions Handout
	2. Making and Recording Notes	
	3. Framing Inquiry	
III. DEEPENING UNDERSTANDING *I analyze key sources to deepen my understanding and answer my Inquiry Questions.*	**1. Selecting Key Sources**	Potential Sources Assessing Sources Handout Taking Notes Forming Evidence-Based Claims Student Research Literacy Skills and Discussion Habits Checklist Connecting Ideas Handout
	2. Analyzing Researched Information	
	3. Writing Evidence-Based Claims	
IV. FINALIZING INQUIRY *I synthesize my information to determine what I have learned and what more I need to know about my area of investigation. I gather and analyze more information to complete my inquiry.*	**1. Organizing Evidence**	Research Frame Forming Evidence-Based Claims Organizing Evidence-Based Claims Student Research Literacy Skills and Discussion Habits Checklist *Repeat Parts II and III*
	2. Evaluating Research	
	3. Refining and Extending Inquiry	
V. DEVELOPING AND COMMUNICATING AN EVIDENCE-BASED PERSPECTIVE *I review and synthesize my research to develop and communicate an evidence-based perspective on my area of investigation.*	**1. Reviewing Research**	Research Frame Organizing Evidence-Based Claims Student Research Literacy Skills and Discussion Habits Checklist Connecting Ideas Handout
	2. Expressing an Evidence-Based Perspective	
	3. Communicating an Evidence-Based Perspective	

STUDENT RESEARCH PORTFOLIO DESCRIPTION

The research portfolio helps you store and organize your findings and analysis throughout every step of the research process. Various tools help you develop a research strategy and record, analyze, and annotate your sources. Every time you complete a tool or annotate a source, file it in the corresponding section of your portfolio. Keeping an organized portfolio helps you make connections, see what you already have, and determine what you still have left to investigate. It will also provide everything you need to write your conclusions when you finish your research. The portfolio may be in either electronic or paper format.

PORTFOLIO SECTIONS	CONTENT
SECTION 1: DEFINING AN AREA OF INVESTIGATION *This section stores all the work you do exploring the topic and choosing an area of investigation.*	Exploring a Topic Area Evaluation Checklist
SECTION 2: GATHERING AND ANALYZING INFORMATION *This section stores all the information you gather throughout your investigation. It also stores your notes and analysis of sources.* *All the tools should be grouped by source.*	Potential Sources Annotated Sources Personal Drafts Taking Notes (about sources) Forming Evidence-Based Claims
SECTION 3: DRAWING CONCLUSIONS *This section stores your notes and Evidence-Based Claims about Inquiry Paths, your research evaluations, and the personal perspective that you come to at the end of your inquiry.* *Group the Taking Notes, Forming Evidence-Based Claim, or Organizing Evidence-Based Claim by Inquiry Path.*	Taking Notes (about Inquiry Paths) Forming Evidence-Based Claims Organizing Evidence-Based Claims Research Evaluation
SECTION 4: DISCARDED MATERIAL *This section stores all the sources and analysis that you have discarded throughout your investigation.* *The purpose of this section is to keep a record of discarded materials until the end of the research process in case you change your mind and want to use them.*	

POSING INQUIRY QUESTIONS

Successful research results from posing good Inquiry Questions. When you have to solve a difficult problem or want to investigate a complex idea or issue, **developing questions about things you need to know helps guide your research and analysis**. But not all questions are created equal. Some lead to dead ends, and others open up vistas of knowledge and understanding … or best of all: more questions!

GENERATING QUESTIONS

Generating questions is most fun and effective with friends—the more minds the merrier. And **starting with lots of questions** helps you find the best ones. When brainstorming questions, consider many things about your Area of Investigation, for instance:

- **How is it defined?**
- **Where did it originate?**
- **What is its history?**
- **What are its major aspects?**
- **What are its causes and implications?**
- **What other things is it connected to or associated with?**
- **What are its important places, things, people, and experts?**

SELECTING AND REFINING QUESTIONS

Once you have a huge list of possible questions, select and refine them by asking yourself a few things about them:

Are you genuinely interested in answering your question?

Research requires hard work and endurance. If you don't care about your questions you won't do the work to answer them. The best questions are about things you actually want and need to know.

Can your question truly be answered through your research?

Some questions are unanswerable (How many walnuts are there in the world?) or take years to answer (What is the meaning of life?). Your Inquiry Questions must put you on a reachable path.

Is your question clear?

Can you pose your question in a way that you and others understand what you are asking? If it's confusing, then perhaps you are asking more than one thing. That's great: just break it into two questions. The more good Inquiry Questions you have the better.

What sort of answers does your question require?

Interesting, meaningful research comes from interesting questions. Good Inquiry Questions are rich enough to support lots of investigation that may even lead to multiple answers and more questions. Questions that can be answered with a simple yes or no generally do not make good Inquiry Questions.

Do you already know what the answer is?

Good Inquiry Questions are actually questions. If you already have answered the questions for yourself, then you won't really be inquiring through your research. If you already know what you think, then you won't get the true reward of research: a deeper knowledge and understanding of things you want to know about.

ASSESSING SOURCES

ASSESSING A SOURCE'S ACCESSIBILITY AND INTEREST LEVEL

Consider your initial experience in reading the text, how well you understand it, and whether it seems interesting to you:

ACCESSIBILITY TO YOU AS A READER	INTEREST AND MEANING FOR YOU AS A READER
• Am I able to read and comprehend the text easily? • How do the text's structure and formatting either help or hinder me in reading it? • Do I have adequate background knowledge to understand the terminology, information, and ideas in the text?	• Does the text present ideas or information that I find interesting? • Which of my Inquiry Paths will the text provide information for? • Which Inquiry Questions does the text help me answer? How?

ASSESSING A SOURCE'S CREDIBILITY

Look at the information you can find about the text in the following areas, and consider the following questions to assess a source text's credibility:

PUBLISHER	DATE	AUTHOR	TYPE
• What is the publisher's relationship to the topic area? • What economic stake might the publisher have in the topic area? • What political stake might the publisher have in the topic area?	• When was the text first published? • How current is the information on the topic? • How does the publishing date relate to the history of the topic?	• What are the author's qualifications or credentials relative to the topic area? • What is the author's personal relationship to the topic area? • What economic or political stakes might the author have in the topic area?	• What type of text is it: explanation, informational article, feature, research study, op-ed, essay, argument, other? • What is the purpose of the text with respect to the topic area?

ASSESSING A SOURCE'S RELEVANCE AND RICHNESS

Using your research frame as a reference, consider the following questions:

RELEVANCE TO TOPIC AND PURPOSE	RELEVANCE TO AREA OF INVESTIGATION	SCOPE AND RICHNESS
• What information does the text provide on the topic? • How might the text help me accomplish the purpose for my research? • Does the text provide accurate information?	• How is the text related to the specific area I am investigating? • Which of my Paths of Inquiry might the text provide information for? • Which Inquiry Questions might the text help me address? How?	• How long is the text and what is the scope of the topic areas it addresses? • How extensive and supported is the information it provides? • How does the information in the text relate to other texts?

CONNECTING IDEAS

USING TRANSITIONAL WORDS AND PHRASES

Transitional words and phrases create links between your ideas when you are speaking and writing. They help your audience understand the logic of your thoughts. When using transitional words, make sure that they are the right match for what you want to express. And remember, transition words work best when they are connecting two or more strong ideas that are clearly stated. Here is a list of transitional words and phrases that you can use for different purposes.

ADD RELATED INFORMATION	GIVE AN EXAMPLE OR ILLUSTRATE AN IDEA	MAKE SURE YOUR THINKING IS CLEARLY UNDERSTOOD	COMPARE IDEAS OR SHOW HOW IDEAS ARE SIMILAR	CONTRAST IDEAS OR SHOW HOW THEY ARE DIFFERENT
• furthermore • moreover • too • also • again • in addition • next • further • finally • and, or, nor	• to illustrate • to demonstrate • specifically • for instance • as an illustration • for example	• that is to say • in other words • to explain • i.e., (that is) • to clarify • to rephrase it • to put it another way	• in the same way • by the same token • similarly • in like manner • likewise • in similar fashion	• nevertheless • but • however • otherwise • on the contrary • in contrast • on the other hand

EXPLAIN HOW ONE THING CAUSES ANOTHER	EXPLAIN THE EFFECT OR RESULT OF SOMETHING	EXPLAIN YOUR PURPOSE	LIST RELATED INFORMATION	QUALIFY SOMETHING
• because • since • on account of • for that reason	• therefore • consequently • accordingly • thus • hence • as a result	• in order that • so that • to that end, to this end • for this purpose • for this reason	• First, second, third … • First, then, also, finally	• almost • nearly • probably • never • always • frequently • perhaps • maybe

ODELL EDUCATION

RESEARCHING TO DEEPEN UNDERSTANDING—FINAL WRITING TASK

In this unit, you have been developing your skills as a **researcher** by:

- Exploring a topic with your learning community
- Posing inquiry questions
- Assessing and analyzing sources
- Making claims about sources
- Maintaining an organized Research Portfolio
- Developing an Evidence-Based Perspective on the topic

Now you will have an opportunity to share what you've learned in a short reflective research narrative. Your narrative should clearly express your understanding of the topic and "tell the story" of how you have developed your new knowledge. *It does not need to fully summarize and include all of your research.*

FINAL ASSIGNMENT: REFLECTIVE RESEARCH NARRATIVE

In the reflective research narrative you will:

- tell a story about what you've learned about the topic through your investigation
- use notes and claims from your portfolio that you have already written
- clearly connect your ideas to the sources where you have found them
- reflect on what you have learned about the research process

To write this narrative, you will:

1. Review your Research Portfolio.
   a. Review the materials you have compiled and organized in your Research Portfolio:
      - *Taking Notes Tools*
      - *Forming EBC-Research Tools*
      - *Organizing EBC-Research Tools*
      - *Written EBC(s)*
   b. Identify key materials that have helped you develop you thinking about the topic.
   c. Arrange key materials in a chronological order, to help you organize the narrative you will write.
2. Think of several different ways you and your classmates have come to understand the topic of "Water: Why is it so valuable?" based on the texts you have read.
   a. Select one or two of these ideas that match your own understanding, and return to the question:
      What do I think about this aspect of the topic of Water?

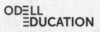

FINAL WRITING TASK (Continued)

   b. Your response can be used as an evidence-based perspective that you can work into your narrative.

3. Think further about your perspective and your research by considering and discussing any of the following questions:

   a. Before starting my inquiry, what did I think about the topic? How did I view or understand it?

   b. What specific steps did I take to research the topic? How did I address and answer my Inquiry Questions?

   c. Which sources were the most interesting to me and why? What specifically did I find interesting about the sources?

   d. What did I learn and discover about my Area of Investigation and Inquiry Question(s)?

   e. What Inquiry Questions did I research that did not lead me anywhere?

   f. What did I learn from my peers about the topic?

   g. What moments were key in developing my understanding of the topic? When did I "get" something major about the topic?

   h. What do I now think about the topic I have investigated, based on the research and reading I have done? What is my own perspective?

   i. What did I learn about the research process? Where did I struggle and where did I triumph?

4. Develop an outline of your reflective research narrative.

   a. Think about telling the story of how you reached your perspective in a *chronological order*, from what you first thought or knew, through what you did to learn more about the topic, to how you arrived at your new understanding and perspective.

   b. Use your **Forming EBC Tools**, Written EBCs, and **Organizing EBC Tools** to develop a detailed plan for your narrative.

5. Write a first draft of your reflective research narrative.

   a. Tell the story of how you researched the topic and arrived at your new perspective on it.

   b. Use your **Taking Notes Tools** to include evidence from relevant texts to support your story and your claims, accurately quoting and paraphrasing.

   c. Tell your story in the first person ("I"), present interesting details to help your reader understand it, and make good word choices to express and connect your ideas.

   d. Your reflective research narrative should do the following things, which will be evaluated in your final draft:

      ⇒ Express your original understanding of the research topic and tell the story of how you arrived at your new understanding.

      ⇒ Communicate a new perspective on the topic that is clearly connected to the area of investigation and supported by your research.

      ⇒ Explain and support the new perspective by discussing claims you have derived from inquiry questions.

      ⇒ Discuss evidence from relevant texts by accurately quoting and paraphrasing.

      ⇒ Use a clear narrative structure to sequence sentences and paragraphs and to present a coherent explanation of the perspective.

FINAL WRITING TASK (Continued)

⇒ Use an informal narrative voice (first person) and effective words and phrases to communicate and connect ideas.

⇒ Present your reflections on what you have learned about the research process, using specific terminology from the unit.

6. Work with other students to review and improve your reflective research narrative.

   a. Use the following Guiding Review Questions to guide self- and peer reviews of your narrative:

   ⇒ *Do I reflect on how I originally thought of the topic before I started to research it?*

   ⇒ *Do I recount the specific steps I took to think of Inquiry Questions around the Area of Investigation?*

   ⇒ *Do I tell how I read and analyzed texts to help answer my Inquiry Questions?*

   ⇒ *Do I clearly communicate how I arrived at my research-based perspective?*

   ⇒ *What is the perspective and is it clearly stated?*

   ⇒ *Are the claims I present in my narrative "well supported," and is there enough evidence to explain or defend my perspective?*

   ⇒ *Are the sources cited accurately and consistently?*

   ⇒ *What can be added or revised to better express the perspective?*

7. Complete any additional drafts and peer reviews of your paper as instructed.

SKILLS AND HABITS TO BE DEMONSTRATED:

As you develop a fine-tuned perspective on the topic, think about demonstrating the Literacy Skills and Academic Habits listed below to the best of your ability. Your teacher will evaluate your work and determine your grade based on how well you:

- **IDENTIFY RELATIONSHIPS:** Notice important connections among details, ideas, and texts

- **MAKE INFERENCES:** Draw sound conclusions from examining a text closely

- **SUMMARIZE:** Correctly explain what a text says about a topic

- **QUESTION:** Develop questions and lines of inquiry that lead to important ideas

- **RECOGNIZE PERSPECTIVE:** Identify and explain the author's view of the text's topic

- **EVALUATE INFORMATION:** Assess the relevance and credibility of information in sources

- **FORM CLAIMS:** State a meaningful conclusion that is well supported by evidence from sources

- **USE EVIDENCE:** Use well-chosen details from sources to explain and support claims. Accurately paraphrase or quote.

- **ORGANIZE IDEAS:** Organize the narrative and its claims, supporting ideas, and evidence in a logical order

- **PRESENT DETAILS:** Describe and explain important details to tell the story

- **PUBLISH:** Use effective formatting and citations when paraphrasing, quoting, and listing sources

- **REFLECT CRITICALLY:** Use research concepts and terms to discuss and evaluate learning

ODELL
EDUCATION

FINAL WRITING TASK (Continued)

SKILLS AND HABITS TO BE DEMONSTRATED (Continued)

- **GENERATE IDEAS:** Generate and develop ideas, perspectives, products, and solutions to problems
- **ORGANIZE WORK:** Maintain materials so that they can be used effectively and efficiently
- **COMPLETE TASKS:** Finish short and extended tasks by established deadlines
- **UNDERSTAND PURPOSE AND PROCESS:** Understand why and how a task should be accomplished

NOTE

These skills and habits are also listed on the *Student Literacy Skills and Academic Habits Checklist* in your **Literacy Toolbox**, which you can use to assess your work and the work of other students.

INITIATING INQUIRY

Overview and Tools

OBJECTIVE:	To learn about inquiry and research. You initially explore a topic and build background knowledge through reading and discussion. Then you will begin your inquiry by coming up with questions to direct your research. By the end of Part 1, you will have chosen an area of investigation and developed one or more Inquiry Questions.

MATERIALS:
- *Student Research Plan*
- *Questioning Path Tool (Reading Closely Literacy Toolbox)*
- *Exploring a Topic Tool*
- *Guiding Questions Handout (Reading Closely Literacy Toolbox)*

- *Potential Sources Tool*
- *Area Evaluation Checklist*
- *Posing Inquiry Questions Handout*

COMMON SOURCES
Common Sources 1 through 4

ACTIVITIES

1. INTRODUCTION TO THE UNIT
Your teacher explains how critical readers use research to deepen their understanding and develop an evidence-based perspective on a topic. You are introduced to the purposes, the process, and the products of the unit.

2. EXPLORING A TOPIC
Your teacher leads a class exploration of a topic. You independently explore the research topic.

3. CONDUCTING PRE-SEARCHES
You conduct pre-searches for sources about one or two Areas of Investigation.

4. VETTING AREAS OF INVESTIGATION
You evaluate your potential Areas of Investigation and develop a research question or problem.

5. GENERATING INQUIRY QUESTIONS
You generate Inquiry Questions to guide your searches for information.

APPROACHING TEXTS TOOL

Name _____ Text _____

APPROACHING THE TEXT

Before reading, I consider what my specific purposes for reading are.

What are my reading purposes?

I also take note of key information about the text.

Title:

Author:

Source/Publisher:

Text type:

Publication date:

What do I already think or understand about the text based on this information?

QUESTIONING THE TEXT

As I read the text for the first time, I use Guiding Questions that relate to my reading purpose and focus. (Can be taken from the Guiding Questions Handout.)

Guiding Questions for *my first reading* of the text:

As I read I mark details on the text that relate to my Guiding Questions.

As I reread, I use questions I have about specific details that have emerged in my reading to focus my analysis and deepen my understanding.

Text-specific questions to help focus *my rereading* of the text:

ODELL EDUCATION

QUESTIONING PATH TOOL

Name: _____ **Text:** _____

APPROACHING:
I determine my reading purposes and take note of key information about the text. I identify the LIPS domain(s) that will guide my initial reading.

Purpose:

Key information:

LIPS domain(s):

QUESTIONING: *I use Guiding Questions to help me investigate the text (from the **Guiding Questions Handout**).*

1.

2.

ANALYZING: *I question further to connect and analyze the details I find (from the **Guiding Questions Handout**).*

1.

2.

DEEPENING: *I consider the questions of others.*

1.

2.

3.

EXTENDING: *I pose my own questions.*

1.

2.

ODELL EDUCATION

ANALYZING DETAILS TOOL

Name _____

Text _ _ _ _ _ _ _ _ _ _ _ _ _

Reading purpose:

A question I have about the text:

SEARCHING FOR DETAILS

I read the text closely and mark words and phrases that help me think about my question.

SELECTING DETAILS

I select words or phrases from my search that I think are the most important in thinking about my question.

Detail 1 (Ref.:)	Detail 2 (Ref.:)	Detail 3 (Ref.:)

ANALYZING DETAILS

I reread parts of the text and think about the meaning of the details and what they tell me about my question.

What I think about detail 1:	What I think about detail 2:	What I think about detail 3:

CONNECTING DETAILS

I compare the details and explain the connections I see among them.

How I connect the details:

ODELL
EDUCATION

EXPLORING A TOPIC TOOL

Name _ _ _ _ _ _ _ _ _ _ **Topic** _ _ _ _ _ _ _ _ _

Write a brief account of the class conversation about the topic
describing what you know at this point about some of its aspects:

POTENTIAL AREA OF INVESTIGATION 1
In a few words, describe an area within the topic that you would like to know more about:
Explain why you are interested in this area of the topic:
Express your potential Area of Investigation as a question or problem:

ODELL
EDUCATION

EXPLORING A TOPIC TOOL

Name _____   **Topic** _____

POTENTIAL AREA OF INVESTIGATION 1	POTENTIAL AREA OF INVESTIGATION 2	POTENTIAL AREA OF INVESTIGATION 3	POTENTIAL AREA OF INVESTIGATION 4
In a few words, describe what you would like to know more about within the topic:	In a few words, describe what you would like to know more about within the topic:	In a few words, describe what you would like to know more about within the topic:	In a few words, describe what you would like to know more about within the topic:
Explain why you are interested in this:	Explain why you are interested in this:	Explain why you are interested in this:	Explain why you are interested in this:
Express your potential area of investigation as a question or problem:	Express your potential area of investigation as a question or problem:	Express your potential area of investigation as a question or problem:	Express your potential area of investigation as a question or problem:

ODELL EDUCATION

POTENTIAL SOURCES TOOL

Name _ _ _ _ _ _ _ _ _ _ _ _ _ _ _ **Topic** _ _ _ _ _ _ _ _ _ _ _ _ _ _

Area of Investigation _

SOURCE	Title:		Location:	
No.		Author:	Text type:	Publication date:

General Content/Key Ideas/Personal Comments:

Connection to Inquiry Paths:

Accessibility/Interest: [ ] High [ ] Medium [ ] Low Credibility: [ ] High [ ] Medium [ ] Low Relevance/Richness: [ ] High [ ] Medium [ ] Low

SOURCE	Title:		Location:	
No.		Author:	Text type:	Publication date:

General Content/Key Ideas/Personal Comments:

Connection to Inquiry Paths:

Accessibility/Interest: [ ] High [ ] Medium [ ] Low Credibility: [ ] High [ ] Medium [ ] Low Relevance/Richness: [ ] High [ ] Medium [ ] Low

SOURCE	Title:		Location:	
No.		Author:	Text type:	Publication date:

General Content/Key Ideas/Personal Comments:

Connection to Inquiry Paths:

Accessibility/Interest: [ ] High [ ] Medium [ ] Low Credibility: [ ] High [ ] Medium [ ] Low Relevance/Richness: [ ] High [ ] Medium [ ] Low

ODELL EDUCATION

POTENTIAL SOURCES TOOL

Name _ _ _ _ _ _ _ _ _ _ _ _ _ _ _ **Topic** _ _ _ _ _ _ _ _ _ _ _ _ _ _ _ _ _ _

Area of Investigation _

SOURCE		
No.	Title:	Location:
	Author:	Publication date:
		Text type:
General Content/Key Ideas/Personal Comments:		Connection to Inquiry Paths:
Accessibility/Interest: [ ] High [ ] Medium [ ] Low	Credibility: [ ] High [ ] Medium [ ] Low	Relevance/Richness: [ ] High [ ] Medium [ ] Low

SOURCE		
No.	Title:	Location:
	Author:	Publication date:
		Text type:
General Content/Key Ideas/Personal Comments:		Connection to Inquiry Paths:
Accessibility/Interest: [ ] High [ ] Medium [ ] Low	Credibility: [ ] High [ ] Medium [ ] Low	Relevance/Richness: [ ] High [ ] Medium [ ] Low

SOURCE		
No.	Title:	Location:
	Author:	Publication date:
		Text type:
General Content/Key Ideas/Personal Comments:		Connection to Inquiry Paths:
Accessibility/Interest: [ ] High [ ] Medium [ ] Low	Credibility: [ ] High [ ] Medium [ ] Low	Relevance/Richness: [ ] High [ ] Medium [ ] Low

ODELL EDUCATION

POTENTIAL SOURCES TOOL

Name _ _ _ _ _ _ _ _ _ _ **Topic** _ _ _ _ _ _ _ _ _ _

Area of Investigation _ _ _ _ _ _ _ _ _ _

SOURCE

| No. | Title: | Location: |
| | Author: | Publication date: |

Text type:

General Content/Key Ideas/Personal Comments:

Connection to Inquiry Paths:

Accessibility/Interest: [ ] High [ ] Medium [ ] Low | Credibility: [ ] High [ ] Medium [ ] Low | Relevance/Richness: [ ] High [ ] Medium [ ] Low

SOURCE

| No. | Title: | Location: |
| | Author: | Publication date: |

Text type:

General Content/Key Ideas/Personal Comments:

Connection to Inquiry Paths:

Accessibility/Interest: [ ] High [ ] Medium [ ] Low | Credibility: [ ] High [ ] Medium [ ] Low | Relevance/Richness: [ ] High [ ] Medium [ ] Low

SOURCE

| No. | Title: | Location: |
| | Author: | Publication date: |

Text type:

General Content/Key Ideas/Personal Comments:

Connection to Inquiry Paths:

Accessibility/Interest: [ ] High [ ] Medium [ ] Low | Credibility: [ ] High [ ] Medium [ ] Low | Relevance/Richness: [ ] High [ ] Medium [ ] Low

ODELL EDUCATION

ANALYZING DETAILS TOOL

Name _____

Text _____

Reading purpose:

A question I have about the text:

SEARCHING FOR DETAILS

I read the text closely and mark words and phrases that help me think about my question.

SELECTING DETAILS

I select words or phrases from my search that I think are the most important in thinking about my question.

Detail 1 (Ref.:)	Detail 2 (Ref.:)	Detail 3 (Ref.:)

ANALYZING DETAILS

I reread parts of the text and think about the meaning of the details and what they tell me about my question.

What I think about detail 1:	What I think about detail 2:	What I think about detail 3:

CONNECTING DETAILS

I compare the details and explain the connections I see among them.

How I connect the details:

ODELL EDUCATION

PART 2

GATHERING INFORMATION

Overview and Tools

OBJECTIVE:	You learn how to conduct searches, assess and annotate sources, and keep an organized record of your findings. By the end of Part 2, you will have framed your inquiry and gathered your main body of research material.

MATERIALS:
- *Student-identified sources*
- *Potential Sources Tool*
- *Assessing Sources Handout*
- *Taking Notes Tool*

- *Posing Inquiry Questions Handout*
- *Research Frame Tool*

COMMON SOURCES:
- **Common Sources 1 through 4**

ACTIVITIES

1. PLANNING SEARCHES FOR INFORMATION
Your teacher works with you to determine how to organize your search and where to look for the information you need.

2. BUILDING AN INITIAL RESEARCH FRAME
You develop an initial plan to organize your research.

3. CONDUCTING SEARCHES FOR BACKGROUND SOURCES USING INQUIRY QUESTIONS AND PATHS
You use inquiry questions to help you look for sources that can help you better understand your topic.

4. ASSESSING SOURCES
Your teacher explains how to assess sources to determine their credibility and relevance to your Inquiry Questions.

5. MAKING AND RECORDING NOTES
Your teacher explains how to annotate sources and record key information and ideas as you conduct your research.

6. CONDUCTING SEARCHES INDEPENDENTLY
You use inquiry questions to conduct strategic searches for potential sources, annotating, making, and recording notes.

7. REVIEWING AND REVISING THE RESEARCH FRAME
You reflect on how your research is going and make adjustments to your strategy.

ODELL
EDUCATION

RESEARCH FRAME TOOL

Name _ **Topic** _

Area of Investigation _ _ _ _ _ _ _ _ _ _ _ _ _ _ _ _ _ _

INQUIRY PATH	INQUIRY PATH	INQUIRY PATH
Reference: IP No.	Reference: IP No.	Reference: IP No.
Name this Inquiry Path in the form of a brief description or question:	Name this Inquiry Path in the form of a brief description or question:	Name this Inquiry Path in the form of a brief description or question:
List all the questions in this Inquiry Path:	List all the questions in this Inquiry Path:	List all the questions in this Inquiry Path:

POTENTIAL SOURCES TOOL

Name _____   **Topic** _____

Area of Investigation _____

SOURCE	Title:	Location:
No.	Author:	Publication date:

General Content/Key Ideas/Personal Comments:

Connection to Inquiry Paths:

Accessibility/Interest: [ ] High [ ] Medium [ ] Low   Credibility: [ ] High [ ] Medium [ ] Low   Relevance/Richness: [ ] High [ ] Medium [ ] Low

SOURCE	Title:	Location:
No.	Author:	Publication date:

General Content/Key Ideas/Personal Comments:

Connection to Inquiry Paths:

Accessibility/Interest: [ ] High [ ] Medium [ ] Low   Credibility: [ ] High [ ] Medium [ ] Low   Relevance/Richness: [ ] High [ ] Medium [ ] Low

SOURCE	Title:	Location:
No.	Author:	Publication date:

General Content/Key Ideas/Personal Comments:

Connection to Inquiry Paths:

Accessibility/Interest: [ ] High [ ] Medium [ ] Low   Credibility: [ ] High [ ] Medium [ ] Low   Relevance/Richness: [ ] High [ ] Medium [ ] Low

TAKING NOTES TOOL

Name _

Source(s) _

Inquiry Question/Path _ _ _ _ _ _ _ _ _ _ _

REFERENCE	DETAILS	COMMENTS
Source no. and location in the source:	I record details, ideas, or information that I find in my sources that help me answer my Inquiry Questions:	I explain the reason why I think they are important and write personal comments:

TAKING NOTES TOOL

Name _

Source(s) _

Inquiry Question/Path _ _ _ _ _ _ _ _ _ _ _ _ _ _ _

REFERENCE	DETAILS	COMMENTS
Source no. and location in the source:	*I record details, ideas, or information that I find in my sources that help me answer my Inquiry Questions:*	*I explain the reason why I think they are important and write personal comments:*

ODELL
EDUCATION

TAKING NOTES TOOL

Name _

Source(s) _

Inquiry Question/Path _ _ _ _ _ _ _ _ _ _ _ _ _ _ _

REFERENCE	DETAILS	COMMENTS
Source no. and location in the source:	I record details, ideas, or information that I find in my sources that help me answer my Inquiry Questions:	I explain the reason why I think they are important and write personal comments:

TAKING NOTES TOOL

Name _

Source(s) _

Inquiry Question/Path _ _ _ _ _ _ _ _ _ _ _ _ _ _

REFERENCE	DETAILS	COMMENTS
Source no. and location in the source:	I record details, ideas, or information that I find in my sources that help me answer my Inquiry Questions:	I explain the reason why I think they are important and write personal comments:

ODELL
EDUCATION

TAKING NOTES TOOL

Name _

Source(s) _ _ _ _ _ _ _ _ _ _ _ _ _ _ _ _ _ _ _

Inquiry Question/Path _ _ _ _ _ _ _ _ _ _ _ _

REFERENCE	DETAILS	COMMENTS
Source no. and location in the source:	*I record details, ideas, or information that I find in my sources that help me answer my Inquiry Questions:*	*I explain the reason why I think they are important and write personal comments:*

TAKING NOTES TOOL

Name _

Source(s) _ _ _ _ _ _ _ _ _ _ _ _ _ _ _ _ _ _ _

Inquiry Question/Path _ _ _ _ _ _ _ _ _ _ _

REFERENCE	DETAILS	COMMENTS
Source no. and location in the source:	*I record details, ideas, or information that I find in my sources that help me answer my Inquiry Questions:*	*I explain the reason why I think they are important and write personal comments:*

ODELL EDUCATION

TAKING NOTES TOOL

Name _

Source(s) _ _ _ _ _ _ _ _ _ _ _ _ _ _ _ _ _ _ _

Inquiry Question/Path _ _ _ _ _ _ _ _ _ _ _ _

REFERENCE	DETAILS	COMMENTS
Source no. and location in the source:	I record details, ideas, or information that I find in my sources that help me answer my Inquiry Questions:	I explain the reason why I think they are important and write personal comments:

RESEARCH FRAME TOOL

Name _____ Topic _____

Area of Investigation _____

INQUIRY PATH	INQUIRY PATH	INQUIRY PATH
Reference: IP No.	**Reference: IP No.**	**Reference: IP No.**
Name this Inquiry Path in the form of a brief description or question:	Name this Inquiry Path in the form of a brief description or question:	Name this Inquiry Path in the form of a brief description or question:
List all the questions in this Inquiry Path:	List all the questions in this Inquiry Path:	List all the questions in this Inquiry Path:

ODELL EDUCATION

RESEARCH FRAME TOOL

Name _ _ _ _ _ _ _ _ _ _ _ **Topic** _ _ _ _ _ _ _ _ _ _ _

Area of Investigation _ _ _ _ _ _ _ _ _ _ _

INQUIRY PATH	INQUIRY PATH	INQUIRY PATH
Reference: IP No.	**Reference: IP No.**	**Reference: IP No.**
Name this Inquiry Path in the form of a brief description or question:	Name this Inquiry Path in the form of a brief description or question:	Name this Inquiry Path in the form of a brief description or question:
List all the questions in this Inquiry Path:	List all the questions in this Inquiry Path:	List all the questions in this Inquiry Path:

PART 3

DEEPENING UNDERSTANDING

Overview and Tools

OBJECTIVE:	You read and analyze key sources closely to deepen your understanding and draw personal conclusions about your area of investigation. By the end of Part 3, you will have a series of evidence-based claims addressing each Inquiry Path of your research frame.

MATERIALS:
- **Student-identified sources**
- *Research Frame Tool*
- *Assessing Sources Handout*
- *Forming EBC Research Tool*
- *Attending to Details Handout*

- *Writing Evidence-Based Claims Handout*
- *Connecting Ideas Handout*

COMMON SOURCES:
- **Common Source 5**

ACTIVITIES

1. SELECTING KEY SOURCES
Your teacher discusses how to identify the most relevant sources and helps you select key sources to analyze through close reading.

2. ANALYZING A SOURCE'S PERSPECTIVE
Your teacher explains how to analyze a source's perspective and relevance to your research and your practice on a source.

3. READING KEY SOURCES CLOSELY—FORMING CLAIMS
You use your Inquiry Questions to read key sources closely, analyzing them for content, perspective, and relevance.

4. WRITING EBCs ABOUT SOURCES
You develop evidence-based summaries and evaluations of key sources using your notes and annotations.

ODELL
EDUCATION

QUESTIONING PATH TOOL

Name: _____ **Text:** _____

APPROACHING: *I determine my reading purposes and take note of key information about the text. I identify the LIPS domain(s) that will guide my initial reading.*	Purpose: Key information: LIPS domain(s):

QUESTIONING: *I use Guiding Questions to help me investigate the text (from the **Guiding Questions Handout**).*

1.

2.

ANALYZING: *I question further to connect and analyze the details I find (from the **Guiding Questions Handout**).*

1.

2.

DEEPENING: *I consider the questions of others.*

1.

2.

3.

EXTENDING: *I pose my own questions.*

1.

2.

ANALYZING DETAILS TOOL

Name _ _ _ _ _ _ _ _ _ _ _ _ _ _ _ **Text** _ _ _ _ _ _ _ _ _ _ _ _ _ _ _

Reading purpose:

A question I have about the text:

SEARCHING FOR DETAILS

I read the text closely and mark words and phrases that help me think about my question.

SELECTING DETAILS	**Detail 1 (Ref.:**)	**Detail 2 (Ref.:**)	**Detail 3 (Ref.:**)
I select words or phrases from my search that I think are the most important in thinking about my question.			

ANALYZING DETAILS

	What I think about detail 1:	**What I think about detail 2:**	**What I think about detail 3:**
I reread parts of the text and think about the meaning of the details and what they tell me about my question.			

CONNECTING DETAILS

	How I connect the details:
I compare the details and explain the connections I see among them.	

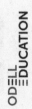

FORMING EVIDENCE-BASED CLAIMS RESEARCH TOOL

Name _____ Source(s) --

Inquiry Question:

SEARCHING FOR DETAILS	I read the sources closely and mark words and phrases that help me answer my question.		
SELECTING DETAILS I select words or phrases from my search that I think are the most important for answering my question. I write the reference next to each detail.	**Detail 1** (Ref.:)	**Detail 2** (Ref.:)	**Detail 3** (Ref.:)

ANALYZING AND CONNECTING DETAILS I reread parts of the texts and think about the meaning of the details and what they tell me about my question. Then I compare the details and explain the connections I see among them.	What I think about the details and how I connect them:

MAKING A CLAIM I state a conclusion I have come to and can support with evidence from the texts after reading them closely.	My claim that answers my Inquiry Question:

FORMING EVIDENCE-BASED CLAIMS RESEARCH TOOL

Name — — — — — — — — — — — — — — — — **Source(s)** — — — — — — — — — — — — — — — —

Inquiry Question:

SEARCHING FOR DETAILS

I read the sources closely and mark words and phrases that help me answer my question.

SELECTING DETAILS

I select words or phrases from my search that I think are the most important for answering my question. I write the reference next to each detail.

Detail 1 (Ref.:)	Detail 2 (Ref.:)	Detail 3 (Ref.:)

ANALYZING AND CONNECTING DETAILS

I reread parts of the texts and think about the meaning of the details and what they tell me about my question. Then I compare the details and explain <u>the connections</u> I see among them.

What I think about the details and how I connect them:

MAKING A CLAIM

I state a conclusion I have come to and can support with <u>evidence</u> from the texts after reading them closely.

My claim that answers my Inquiry Question:

ODELL
EDUCATION

FORMING EVIDENCE-BASED CLAIMS RESEARCH TOOL

Name -

Source(s) -

Inquiry Question:

SEARCHING FOR DETAILS

I read the sources closely and mark words and phrases that help me answer my question.

SELECTING DETAILS

I select words or phrases from my search that I think are the most important for answering my question. I write the reference next to each detail.

Detail 1 (Ref.:)	Detail 2 (Ref.:)	Detail 3 (Ref.:)

ANALYZING AND CONNECTING DETAILS

I reread parts of the texts and think about the meaning of the details and what they tell me about my question. Then I compare the details and explain the connections I see among them.

What I think about the details and how I connect them:

MAKING A CLAIM

I state a conclusion I have come to and can support with evidence from the texts after reading them closely.

My claim that answers my Inquiry Question:

PART 4

FINALIZING INQUIRY

Overview and Tools

OBJECTIVE:	You analyze and evaluate your material with respect to your Inquiry Questions and refine and complete your research. By the end of Part 4, you will have an analyzed body of research addressing your Inquiry Questions from which to develop and communicate an evidence-based perspective on the area of investigation.

MATERIALS:
- *Research Frame Tool*
- *Forming EBC Research Tool*
- *Organizing EBC Research Tool*
- *Connecting Ideas Handout*
- *Research Evaluation Tool*

ACTIVITIES

1. ADDRESSING INQUIRY PATHS
You review your notes and analysis across the sources to address one of your Inquiry Paths.

2. ORGANIZING EVIDENCE
You review and organize your research and analysis, establishing connections to address all the Inquiry Paths of your research frame.

3. EVALUATING RESEARCH
You review and discuss your research frames and researched materials to determine relevance, coherence, and sufficiency.

4. REFINING AND EXTENDING INQUIRY
You refine and extend your scope of inquiry based on teacher and peer feedback.

ODELL
EDUCATION

ORGANIZING EVIDENCE-BASED CLAIMS
RESEARCH TOOL (2 POINTS)

Name – – – – – – – – – – – – – – Inquiry Path – – – – – – – – – – – –

CLAIM:

Point 1

A Supporting Evidence	B Supporting Evidence
(Reference:)	(Reference:)
C Supporting Evidence	D Supporting Evidence
(Reference:)	(Reference:)

Point 2

A Supporting Evidence	B Supporting Evidence
(Reference:)	(Reference:)
C Supporting Evidence	D Supporting Evidence
(Reference:)	(Reference:)

ODELL EDUCATION

ORGANIZING EVIDENCE-BASED CLAIMS RESEARCH TOOL (3 POINTS)

Name _ _ _ _ _ _ _ _ _ _ _ _ _ _ _ _ _ _ — — — Inquiry Path — — —

CLAIM:

Point 1

A	Supporting Evidence
(Reference:	)
B	Supporting Evidence
(Reference:	)
C	Supporting Evidence
(Reference:	)

Point 2

A	Supporting Evidence
(Reference:	)
B	Supporting Evidence
(Reference:	)
C	Supporting Evidence
(Reference:	)

Point 3

A	Supporting Evidence
(Reference:	)
B	Supporting Evidence
(Reference:	)
C	Supporting Evidence
(Reference:	)

ODELL EDUCATION

ORGANIZING EVIDENCE-BASED CLAIMS
RESEARCH TOOL (2 POINTS)

Name _____

-------- Inquiry Path --------

CLAIM:

Point 1

Point 2

| **A** Supporting Evidence | **B** Supporting Evidence |
| | |

(Reference:)

| **A** Supporting Evidence | **B** Supporting Evidence |
| | |

(Reference:)

| **C** Supporting Evidence | **D** Supporting Evidence |
| | |

(Reference:)

| **C** Supporting Evidence | **D** Supporting Evidence |
| | |

(Reference:)

ODELL EDUCATION

ORGANIZING EVIDENCE-BASED CLAIMS
RESEARCH TOOL (3 POINTS)

Name _____ Inquiry Path

CLAIM:

Point 1

A   Supporting Evidence

(Reference:)

B   Supporting Evidence

(Reference:)

C   Supporting Evidence

(Reference:)

Point 2

A   Supporting Evidence

(Reference:)

B   Supporting Evidence

(Reference:)

C   Supporting Evidence

(Reference:)

Point 3

A   Supporting Evidence

(Reference:)

B   Supporting Evidence

(Reference:)

C   Supporting Evidence

(Reference:)

ORGANIZING EVIDENCE-BASED CLAIMS
RESEARCH TOOL (2 POINTS)

Name _____   - - - - - - - Inquiry Path - - - - - - -

CLAIM:

Point 1

A Supporting Evidence	**B** Supporting Evidence
(Reference:)	(Reference:)
C Supporting Evidence	**D** Supporting Evidence
(Reference:)	(Reference:)

Point 2

A Supporting Evidence	**B** Supporting Evidence
(Reference:)	(Reference:)
C Supporting Evidence	**D** Supporting Evidence
(Reference:)	(Reference:)

ODELL EDUCATION

ORGANIZING EVIDENCE-BASED CLAIMS
RESEARCH TOOL (3 POINTS)

Name _   Inquiry Path _ _ _ _ _ _ _ _ _ _ _ _ _ _ _

CLAIM:

Point 1	Point 2	Point 3
A Supporting Evidence	**A** Supporting Evidence	**A** Supporting Evidence
(Reference:)	(Reference:)	(Reference:)
B Supporting Evidence	**B** Supporting Evidence	**B** Supporting Evidence
(Reference:)	(Reference:)	(Reference:)
C Supporting Evidence	**C** Supporting Evidence	**C** Supporting Evidence
(Reference:)	(Reference:)	(Reference:)

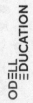

ODELL EDUCATION

FORMING EVIDENCE-BASED CLAIMS RESEARCH TOOL

Name _____

Inquiry Question:

Source(s) _____

SEARCHING FOR DETAILS | I read the sources closely and mark words and phrases that help me answer my question.

SELECTING DETAILS

I select words or phrases from my search that I think are the most important for answering my question. I write the <u>reference</u> next to each detail.

| Detail 1 (Ref.:) | Detail 2 (Ref.:) | Detail 3 (Ref.:) |

ANALYZING AND CONNECTING DETAILS | What I think about the details and how I connect them:

I reread parts of the texts and think about the <u>meaning of the details</u> and what they tell me about my question. Then I compare the details and explain the <u>connections</u> I see among them.

MAKING A CLAIM | My claim that answers my Inquiry Question:

I state a conclusion I have come to and can support with <u>evidence</u> from the texts after reading them closely.

ODELL EDUCATION

PART 1 RESEARCH EVALUATION CRITERIA CHECKLIST

Name _____ Area of Investigation _____ Date ___

RESEARCH EVALUATION CRITERIA CHECKLIST		√	COMMENTS
I. ADEQUACY AND SUFFICIENCY OF RESEARCH *The researcher's investigation follows the Research Frame and the information gathered is sufficient.*	**Adequacy of the research:** The researcher's investigation is based on the Research Frame and the claims and information presented link directly to the Inquiry Paths.	☐	
	Sufficiency of the answers: The answers formulated by the researcher based on his/her investigation are sufficient to cover the scope of each Inquiry Path.	☐	
	Adequacy of the scope and focus of the research: No Inquiry Questions or Paths of the research seem irrelevant with respect to the Research Frame.	☐	
II. CREDIBILITY AND RICHNESS OF SOURCES *The sources gathered by the researcher are credible and rich.*	**Credibility of sources :** The sources gathered by the researcher are credible.	☐	
	Richness of sources: The researcher found a reasonable amount of rich sources that provide important information that is relevant to the inquiry.	☐	
III. RANGE OF PERSPECTIVES *The researcher has considered a wide range of perspectives.*	**Richness of perspectives:** The researcher has considered and explored multiple perspectives.	☐	
	Sufficiency of perspectives: No important perspective has been ignored.	☐	
	Balance among perspectives: There is no over reliance on any one source or perspective.	☐	
IV. COHERENCE OF THE PERSPECTIVE *The EBCs drawn from the analysis of the sources are coherent, sound and supported.*	**Coherence of EBCs:** The evidence-based claims drawn from the analysis of the sources are coherent with respect to the Research Frame.	☐	
	Soundness of EBCs: The evidence-based claim demonstrates knowledge of and sound thinking about the Area of Investigation.	☐	
	Support for EBCs: The evidence-based claims are supported by quotations and examples from the texts.	☐	

ODELL
EDUCATION

PART 2 PEER EVALUATION OF RESEARCH

Presenter: ————————————————— **Reviewer:** —————————————————————

Work in small groups to evaluate each other's research. Rotate roles in your group.

AS A PRESENTER:

- **Present your Area of Investigation and Research Frame.** Describe the general scope of your research and explain why you are interested in this area.

- **Summarize your written claims** for each of your answers to the Inquiry Paths. Make sure you reference evidence from sources to support your claims.

- **Present 2 key sources.** Explain why you think they are key, summarize their content and explain your analysis of these sources to your peers. Explain to your peers your annotations, notes, and EBCs about these sources.

- Make sure you **give your peers the opportunity to ask you questions** during the entire presentation.

- **Take notes** on a Revising Research tool to determine actions you may take to revise your research based on your peers review.

AS A REVIEWER:

- **Listen** carefully to the presentation. **Ask clarifying questions** to the presenter when necessary.

- Using the table below, **make comments and suggestions** about the presentation answering the guiding questions.

GUIDING QUESTIONS	COMMENTS AND SUGGESTIONS
What have you learned about the presenter's area of investigation?	
What was interesting to you in the presentation?	
What new information does the presenter need to find to more fully address existing or new Inquiry Paths?	
What was not clear to you in the presentation?	
What would you like to know more about the presenter's area of investigation?	
Do you have any other comment or suggestions that you think would help the presenter improve his/her work?	

PART 3 REVISING RESEARCH

Presenter:_____ **Reviewer:**_____

Review the feedback on your Research and think about ways you should revise your work. For each action you choose, explain what specific steps you are planning to take.

GUIDING QUESTIONS	MY NOTES, COMMENTS AND FUTURE STEPS
What adjustments and additions do I need to make to my Research Frame?	
Are there sources lacking in credibility that I need to replace?	
What new information do I need to find to more fully address existing or new Inquiry Paths?	
What missing perspectives do I need to research?	
Are there any parts of my research I should discard?	
Other:	

ODELL
EDUCATION

RESEARCH FRAME TOOL

Name — — — — — — — — — — — — — — — — — **Topic** —

Area of Investigation —

INQUIRY PATH	INQUIRY PATH	INQUIRY PATH
Reference: IP No.	**Reference: IP No.**	**Reference: IP No.**
Name this Inquiry Path in the form of a brief description or question:	Name this Inquiry Path in the form of a brief description or question:	Name this Inquiry Path in the form of a brief description or question:
List all the questions in this Inquiry Path:	List all the questions in this Inquiry Path:	List all the questions in this Inquiry Path:

POTENTIAL SOURCES TOOL

Name _ _ _ _ _ _ _ _ _ _ _ _ **Topic** _ _ _ _ _ _ _ _ _ _ _ _ _ _ _ _

Area of Investigation _

SOURCE		
No.	Title:	Location:
	Author:	Text type:
		Publication date:
General Content/Key Ideas/Personal Comments:		Connection to Inquiry Paths:
Accessibility/Interest: [ ] High [ ] Medium [ ] Low	Credibility: [ ] High [ ] Medium [ ] Low	Relevance/Richness: [ ] High [ ] Medium [ ] Low

SOURCE		
No.	Title:	Location:
	Author:	Text type:
		Publication date:
General Content/Key Ideas/Personal Comments:		Connection to Inquiry Paths:
Accessibility/Interest: [ ] High [ ] Medium [ ] Low	Credibility: [ ] High [ ] Medium [ ] Low	Relevance/Richness: [ ] High [ ] Medium [ ] Low

SOURCE		
No.	Title:	Location:
	Author:	Text type:
		Publication date:
General Content/Key Ideas/Personal Comments:		Connection to Inquiry Paths:
Accessibility/Interest: [ ] High [ ] Medium [ ] Low	Credibility: [ ] High [ ] Medium [ ] Low	Relevance/Richness: [ ] High [ ] Medium [ ] Low

ODELL EDUCATION

POTENTIAL SOURCES TOOL

Name _____ **Topic** _____

Area of Investigation _____

SOURCE

No.	Title:	Location:
	Author:	Text type:	Publication date:

General Content/Key Ideas/Personal Comments:

Connection to Inquiry Paths:

Accessibility/Interest: [ ] High [ ] Medium [ ] Low   Credibility: [ ] High [ ] Medium [ ] Low   Relevance/Richness: [ ] High [ ] Medium [ ] Low

SOURCE

No.	Title:	Location:
	Author:	Text type:	Publication date:

General Content/Key Ideas/Personal Comments:

Connection to Inquiry Paths:

Accessibility/Interest: [ ] High [ ] Medium [ ] Low   Credibility: [ ] High [ ] Medium [ ] Low   Relevance/Richness: [ ] High [ ] Medium [ ] Low

SOURCE

No.	Title:	Location:
	Author:	Text type:	Publication date:

General Content/Key Ideas/Personal Comments:

Connection to Inquiry Paths:

Accessibility/Interest: [ ] High [ ] Medium [ ] Low   Credibility: [ ] High [ ] Medium [ ] Low   Relevance/Richness: [ ] High [ ] Medium [ ] Low

ODELL EDUCATION

TAKING NOTES TOOL

Name _

Source(s) _

Inquiry Question/Path _ _ _ _ _ _ _ _ _ _ _ _ _

REFERENCE	DETAILS	COMMENTS
Source no. and location in the source:	I record details, ideas, or information that I find in my sources that help me answer my Inquiry Questions:	I explain the reason why I think they are important and write personal comments:

ODELL EDUCATION

TAKING NOTES TOOL

Name _

Source(s) _

Inquiry Question/Path _ _ _ _ _ _ _ _ _ _ _ _ _

REFERENCE	DETAILS	COMMENTS
Source no. and location in the source:	*I record details, ideas, or information that I find in my sources that help me answer my Inquiry Questions:*	*I explain the reason why I think they are important and write personal comments:*

TAKING NOTES TOOL

Name _

Source(s) _ _ _ _ _ _ _ _ _ _ _ _ _ _ _ _ _ _ _

Inquiry Question/Path _ _ _ _ _ _ _ _ _ _ _

REFERENCE	DETAILS	COMMENTS
Source no. and location in the source:	I record details, ideas, or information that I find in my sources that help me answer my Inquiry Questions:	I explain the reason why I think they are important and write personal comments:

ODELL
EDUCATION

TAKING NOTES TOOL

Name _

Source(s) _ _ _ _ _ _ _ _ _ _ _ _ _ _ _ _ _ _

Inquiry Question/Path _ _ _ _ _ _ _ _ _ _ _

REFERENCE	DETAILS	COMMENTS
Source no. and location in the source:	I record details, ideas, or information that I find in my sources that help me answer my Inquiry Questions:	I explain the reason why I think they are important and write personal comments:

TAKING NOTES TOOL

Name _

Source(s) _

Inquiry Question/Path _ _ _ _ _ _ _ _ _ _ _ _

REFERENCE	DETAILS	COMMENTS
Source no. and location in the source:	*I record details, ideas, or information that I find in my sources that help me answer my Inquiry Questions:*	*I explain the reason why I think they are important and write personal comments:*

ODELL EDUCATION

TAKING NOTES TOOL

Name _

Source(s) _

Inquiry Question/Path _ _ _ _ _ _ _ _ _ _ _ _ _

REFERENCE	DETAILS	COMMENTS
Source no. and location in the source:	I record details, ideas, or information that I find in my sources that help me answer my Inquiry Questions:	I explain the reason why I think they are important and write personal comments:

ORGANIZING EVIDENCE-BASED CLAIMS
RESEARCH TOOL (2 POINTS)

Name _____

- - - - - - - - - - - **Inquiry Path** - - - - - - - - - - -

CLAIM:

Point 1

A Supporting Evidence	**B** Supporting Evidence
(Reference:)	(Reference:)

C Supporting Evidence	**D** Supporting Evidence
(Reference:)	(Reference:)

Point 2

A Supporting Evidence	**B** Supporting Evidence
(Reference:)	(Reference:)

C Supporting Evidence	**D** Supporting Evidence
(Reference:)	(Reference:)

ORGANIZING EVIDENCE-BASED CLAIMS
RESEARCH TOOL (3 POINTS)

Name _ Inquiry Path _ _ _ _ _ _ _ _ _ _ _ _ _

CLAIM:

Point 1	Point 2	Point 3
A Supporting Evidence	**A** Supporting Evidence	**A** Supporting Evidence
(Reference:)	(Reference:)	(Reference:)
B Supporting Evidence	**B** Supporting Evidence	**B** Supporting Evidence
(Reference:)	(Reference:)	(Reference:)
C Supporting Evidence	**C** Supporting Evidence	**C** Supporting Evidence
(Reference:)	(Reference:)	(Reference:)

ORGANIZING EVIDENCE-BASED CLAIMS
RESEARCH TOOL (2 POINTS)

Name _____

----- Inquiry Path -----

CLAIM:

Point 1

A	Supporting Evidence	B	Supporting Evidence

(Reference:)   (Reference:)

C	Supporting Evidence	D	Supporting Evidence

(Reference:)   (Reference:)

Point 2

A	Supporting Evidence	B	Supporting Evidence

(Reference:)   (Reference:)

C	Supporting Evidence	D	Supporting Evidence

(Reference:)   (Reference:)

ODELL EDUCATION

ORGANIZING EVIDENCE-BASED CLAIMS
RESEARCH TOOL (3 POINTS)

Name _____   ----- Inquiry Path -----

CLAIM:

Point 1

A   Supporting Evidence

(Reference: _____)

B   Supporting Evidence

(Reference: _____)

C   Supporting Evidence

(Reference: _____)

Point 2

A   Supporting Evidence

(Reference: _____)

B   Supporting Evidence

(Reference: _____)

C   Supporting Evidence

(Reference: _____)

Point 3

A   Supporting Evidence

(Reference: _____)

B   Supporting Evidence

(Reference: _____)

C   Supporting Evidence

(Reference: _____)

ODELL
EDUCATION

FORMING EVIDENCE-BASED CLAIMS RESEARCH TOOL

Name _____ Source(s) _____

Inquiry Question:

SEARCHING FOR DETAILS

I read the sources closely and mark words and phrases that help me answer my question.

SELECTING DETAILS

I select words or phrases from my search that I think are the most important for answering my question. I write the reference next to each detail.

Detail 1 (Ref.:)	Detail 2 (Ref.:)	Detail 3 (Ref.:)

ANALYZING AND CONNECTING DETAILS

I reread parts of the texts and think about the meaning of the details and what they tell me about my question. Then I compare the details and explain the connections I see among them.

What I think about the details and how I connect them:

MAKING A CLAIM

I state a conclusion I have come to and can support with evidence from the texts after reading them closely.

My claim that answers my Inquiry Question:

ODELL EDUCATION

PART 5

DEVELOPING AND COMMUNICATING AN EVIDENCE-BASED PERSPECTIVE

Overview and Tools

OBJECTIVE: You organize your research and tools to help you write a reflective research narrative on the topic and inquiry experience. You might also express your narrative in a final project such as a multimedia presentation or academic paper.

MATERIALS:
- *Research Frame Tool*
- *Potential Sources Tool*
- *Organizing EBC Research Tool*
- *Connecting Ideas Handout*
- *Writing EBC Handout*
- *Research Evaluation Tool*
- *RDU Final Writing Task Handout*

ACTIVITIES

1. REVIEWING RESEARCH PORTFOLIOS
You review and organize your research portfolios in preparation for communicating your evidence-based perspectives through a reflective research narrative.

2. COMMUNICATING AN EVIDENCE-BASED PERSPECTIVE
You write a reflective research narrative explaining your experience researching your topic and the understanding you have developed.

3. WRITING A BIBLIOGRAPHY
You use your Potential Sources Tools to write a bibliography of your sources.

4. COMMUNICATING A FINAL EVIDENCE-BASED PRODUCT (OPTIONAL)
You develop a multi-media presentation to share your research experience or formal paper to fully communicate your perspective.

AREA EVALUATION CHECKLIST

Date   **Name**   **Area of Investigation**

AREA EVALUATION CHECKLIST		√	COMMENTS
I. COHERENCE OF AREA *What is the Area of Investigation?*	The researcher can speak and write about the Area of Investigation in a way that makes sense to others and is clearly understood.		
II. SCOPE OF AREA *What do I need to know to gain an understanding of the Area of Investigation?*	The questions necessary to investigate for gaining an understanding require more than a quick review of easily accessed sources. The questions are reasonable enough so that the researcher is likely to find credible sources that address the issue in the time allotted for research.		
III. RELEVANCE OF AREA *How is this Area of Investigation related to a larger topic?*	The Area of Investigation is relevant to the larger topic.		
IV. INTEREST IN AREA *Why are you interested in this Area of Investigation?*	The researcher is able to communicate genuine interest in the Area of Investigation. Gaining an understanding of the area would be valuable for the student.		

In one or two sentences express the potential Area of Investigation in the form of a problem or overarching question:

ODELL
EDUCATION

STUDENT RESEARCHING TO DEEPEN UNDERSTANDING SKILLS AND ACADEMIC HABITS CHECKLIST

	RESEARCH LITERACY SKILLS AND ACADEMIC HABITS	✔	Evidence Demonstrating the SKILLS AND HABITS
READING	1. **Identifying Relationships:** Notices important connections among details, ideas, and texts		
	2. **Making Inferences:** Draws sound conclusions from examining a text closely		
	3. **Summarizing:** Correctly explains what a text says about a topic		
	4. **Questioning:** Develops questions and lines of inquiry that lead to important ideas		
THINKING	5. **Recognizing Perspective:** Identifies and explains the author's view of the text's topic		
	6. **Evaluating Information:** Assesses the relevance and credibility of information in sources		
	7. **Forming Claims:** States a meaningful conclusion that is well supported by evidence from sources		
	8. **Using Evidence:** Uses well-chosen details from sources to explain and support claims; accurately paraphrases or quotes		
	9. **Presenting Details:** Describes and explains details that are important in the story of the research process		
	10. **Organizing Ideas:** Organizes the narrative and its claims, supporting ideas, and evidence in a logical order		
	11. **Publishing:** Uses effective formatting and citations when paraphrasing, quoting, and listing sources		
ACADEMIC HABITS	12. **Reflecting Critically:** Uses research concepts and terms to discuss and evaluate learning		
	13. **Generating Ideas:** Generates and develops ideas, perspectives, products, and solutions to problems.		
	14. **Organizing Work:** Maintains materials so that they can be used effectively and efficiently		
	15. **Completing Tasks:** Finishes short and extended tasks by established deadlines		
	16. **Understanding Purpose and Process:** Understands why and how a task should be accomplished		

General comments:

UNIT 4

BUILDING EVIDENCE-BASED ARGUMENTS

DEVELOPING CORE LITERACY PROFICIENCIES

GRADE 7

"Doping can be that last 2 percent"

ODELL
EDUCATION

GOAL

In this unit you will develop your proficiency as a presenter of reasoned arguments. You will learn how to do the following:

1. Understand the background and key aspects of an important issue.
2. Look at various viewpoints on the issue.
3. Read the arguments of others closely and thoughtfully.
4. Develop your own view of the issue and take a stand about it.
5. Make and prove your case by using sound evidence and reasoning to support it.
6. Improve your writing so that others will clearly understand and appreciate your evidence-based argument—and think about the case you have made for it.

TOPIC

In this unit you will learn about the use of performance-enhancing drugs (PEDs) by athletes. You will learn various ways athletes have improved their performance with drugs. As you explore the topic further, you will discover that people do not all agree that this is a good idea. Many leagues and teams restrict athletes from enhancing their performance with drugs. Those who disagree with their use highlight issues of fairness and health. Others believe that the safe use of performance-enhancing drugs is an acceptable development in the history of athletics. You will come up with your own perspective.

ACTIVITIES

You will begin the unit learning about the use of performance-enhancing drugs by athletes. As you begin to understand the issue, you will explore the various perspectives on the use of performance-enhancing drugs. You will then read and analyze a few arguments. After analyzing arguments, you will develop your own position on the issue. Using your notes, you will plan an argument to defend your position. The unit finishes with a collaborative process you will use with your classmates to help you write and revise your final argumentative essay.

BUILDING EVIDENCE-BASED ARGUMENTS LITERACY TOOLBOX

In *Building Evidence-Based Arguments*, you will continue to build your Literacy Toolbox by learning how to use the following handouts, tools, and checklists organized in your Student Edition.

☰ HANDOUTS AND MODEL ARGUMENTS

To support your work with the texts and the tools, you will be able to use the following informational handouts. You may also use handouts from previous Core Proficiencies units:

Guiding Questions Handout

from the *Reading Closely* unit

Connecting Ideas Handout

from the *Research* unit

Evidence-Based Arguments Final Writing Task Handout

This handout gives you a detailed breakdown of the final argumentative essay.

Evidence-Based Arguments Terms

This handout defines the terms used in the unit to talk about and analyze arguments.

Model Arguments

These examples present familiar situations about which people take different positions. You can use these models to practice analyzing arguments.

TOOLS

In addition to using the handouts, you will learn how to use the following tools. You may also use tools from previous Core Proficiencies units:

Analyzing Details Tool

from the *Reading Closely* unit

Questioning Path Tool

from the *Reading Closely* unit

Forming Evidence-Based Claims Tool

from the *Making Evidence-Based Claims* unit

Organizing Evidence-Based Claims Tool

from the *Making Evidence-Based Claims* unit

Delineating Arguments Tool

This tool helps you identify and analyze components of an argument. You can use it to analyze other people's arguments or to help you develop your own.

Evaluating Arguments Tool

This tool helps you evaluate eight characteristics of an argument (some you have seen in the ***Delineating Arguments Tool***): the argument's issue, perspective, credibility and bias, position or thesis, claims, evidence, reasoning and logic, and conclusions. You can also use this tool to rate how convincing the argument is overall.

CHECKLIST

You will also use this checklist throughout the unit to support peer- and self-review:

Building Evidence-Based Arguments Skills and Habits Checklist

This checklist presents and briefly describes the literacy skills and habits you will be working on during the unit. You can use it to remind you of what you are trying to learn; to reflect on what you have done when reading, discussing, or writing; or to give feedback to other students. Your teacher may use it to let you know about your areas of strength and areas in which you need to improve.

BUILDING EVIDENCE-BASED ARGUMENTS UNIT TEXTS

The following table lists the unit texts (organized by numbered text sets) that are used in the activities you will experience as you learn about argumentation. You will read some, but not all, of these texts, depending on decisions your teacher and students in your class make. Additional texts you can read to deepen your understanding are indicated with an "AT."

These texts are accessible on the web for free without any login information, membership requirements, or purchase. Your teacher may provide you with copies of the texts you will read, or you may need to do an Internet search to find them. Because of the ever-changing nature of website addresses, links are not provided. You can locate these texts through web searches using the information provided. To find some of the texts, you may need to use online database portals (e.g., EBSCO, Gale) that are available to teachers and students through your state or district library systems.

TEXT	TITLE	AUTHOR	DATE	SOURCE/PUBLISHER
Text Set 1: Background Informational Texts				
1.1	"What Is a Performance-Enhancing Drug?"	Luke Bauer	12/5/2013	Odell Education
1.2	Historical Timeline: History of Performance Enhancing Drugs in Sports	ProCon.org	8/8/2013	ProCon.org
1.3	"Steroids"	*Kids Health*	2013	*Kids Health*
Text Set 2: Additional Background Informational Texts				
2.1	"How to Get Doping out of Sports"	Jonathan Vaughters	8/11/2012	*New York Times*
2.2	"Performance Enhancing Drugs Outside of Pro Sports"	Kyung Lah	8/5/2013	Anderson Cooper 360, *CNN*
2.3	"Performance Enhancing Drugs: A Cheat Sheet"	Katie Moisse	8/5/2013	*ABC News*
AT	"The Future of Cheating in Sports"	Christie Aschwanden	2012	*Smithsonian Magazine*
AT	"Athlete Guide to the 2013 Prohibited List"	US Anti-Doping Agency	2013	US Anti-Doping Agency
AT	"The Beam in Your Eye"	William Saletan	4/18/2005	*Slate Magazine*
Text Set 3: Political Cartoons				
3.1	Cartoonists on Baseball and Steroids	John Cole; various	6/8/2013	*The Times Tribune* Blogs

		Text Set 4: Seminal Arguments		
4.1	Congressman Elijah E. Cummings Urges the National Basketball Association to Adopt a Zero-Tolerance Drug Policy	Rep. Elijah E. Cummings	5/19/2005	Congressman Elijah E. Cummings House of Representatives site
4.2	Speech by Dr. Jacques Rogge, president, International Olympic Committee to World Conference on Doping in Sport	Dr. Jacques Rogge	11/15/2007	International Olympic Committee
4.3	"Why It's Time to Legalize Steroids In Professional Sports"	Chris Smith	8/24/2012	Forbes
4.4	"Confessions of a Doper: Lance Armstrong's Former Teammate Jonathan Vaughters Talks about Why Some Athletes Use Steroids."	Jonathan Vaughters	4/11/2012	New York Times Upfront Magazine
		Text Set 5: Additional Arguments		
5.1	"No Place In High School Sports for Performance-Enhancing Drugs"	Roger Dearing	8/20/2013	The News Herald
5.2	"Did Lance Armstrong Cheat? I Don't Care"	LZ Granderson	2/19/2011	ESPN Commentary
5.3	"Lance Armstrong Had Little Choice but to Dope"	John Eustice	10/2/2012	Time Ideas
5.4	"There Are No Sound Moral Arguments Against Performance-Enhancing Drugs"	Chuck Klosterman	10/12/2012	New York Times
AT	"Legalize PEDs and We'll Prosper, Says Ethicist"	Adrian Proszenko	2/17/2013	The Sydney Morning Herald
AT	Why the Use of Performance-Enhancing Drugs by Great Athletes Still Bothers Us	J. Gordon Hylton	NA	Marquette University Law School Blog

BUILDING EVIDENCE-BASED ARGUMENTS

DEVELOPING CORE LITERACY PROFICIENCIES

GRADE 7

Literacy Toolbox

EVIDENCE-BASED ARGUMENTS TERMS

ISSUE	An important aspect of human society for which there are many different opinions about what to think or do; many issues can be framed as a problem-based question
RELATIONSHIP TO ISSUE	A person's particular personal involvement with an issue, given his or her experience, education, occupation, socioeconomic-geographical status, interests, or other characteristics
PERSPECTIVE	How someone understands and views an issue based on his or her current relationship to it and analysis of the issue
POSITION	Someone's stance on what to do or think about a clearly defined issue based on their perspective and understanding of it; when writing argumentative essays, one's position may be expressed as a thesis
THESIS	Another word for *position* sometimes used when writing an argument to support it
IMPLICATIONS	The practical and logical consequences of a position that has been supported by evidence-based argumentation
PREMISES	The claims of an argument that are linked together logically using evidence and reasoning to support a position or thesis
EVIDENCE	The topical and textual facts, events, and ideas from which the premises of an argument arise and are cited to support them
REASONING	The logical relationships among ideas, including claims, premises, and evidence
CHAIN OF REASONING	The logical relationships linking the premises of an argument that lead to the demonstration and support of a position
CLAIM	A personal conclusion about a text, topic, event, or idea
EVIDENCE-BASED CLAIM	A personal conclusion that arises from and is supported by textual and topical evidence

ODELL
EDUCATION

CONNECTING IDEAS

USING TRANSITIONAL WORDS AND PHRASES

Transitional words and phrases create links between your ideas when you are speaking and writing. They help your audience understand the logic of your thoughts. When using transitional words, make sure that they are the right match for what you want to express. And remember, transition words work best when they are connecting two or more strong ideas that are clearly stated. Here is a list of transitional words and phrases that you can use for different purposes.

ADD RELATED INFORMATION	GIVE AN EXAMPLE OR ILLUSTRATE AN IDEA	MAKE SURE YOUR THINKING IS CLEARLY UNDERSTOOD	COMPARE IDEAS OR SHOW HOW IDEAS ARE SIMILAR	CONTRAST IDEAS OR SHOW HOW THEY ARE DIFFERENT
• furthermore • moreover • too • also • again • in addition • next • further • finally • and, or, nor	• to illustrate • to demonstrate • specifically • for instance • as an illustration • for example	• that is to say • in other words • to explain • i.e., (that is) • to clarify • to rephrase it • to put it another way	• in the same way • by the same token • similarly • in like manner • likewise • in similar fashion	• nevertheless • but • however • otherwise • on the contrary • in contrast • on the other hand

EXPLAIN HOW ONE THING CAUSES ANOTHER	EXPLAIN THE EFFECT OR RESULT OF SOMETHING	EXPLAIN YOUR PURPOSE	LIST RELATED INFORMATION	QUALIFY SOMETHING
• because • since • on account of • for that reason	• therefore • consequently • accordingly • thus • hence • as a result	• in order that • so that • to that end, to this end • for this purpose • for this reason	• First, second, third… • First, then, also, finally	• almost • nearly • probably • never • always • frequently • perhaps • maybe

BUILDING EVIDENCE-BASED ARGUMENTS—FINAL WRITING TASK

In this unit, you have been developing your skills as a presenter of reasoned arguments:

- Understanding the background and key aspects of an important issue
- Looking at various viewpoints on the issue
- Reading the arguments of others closely and thoughtfully
- Developing your own view of the issue and taking a position on it
- Making and proving your case by using sound evidence and reasoning to support it
- Improving your thinking and writing so that others will clearly understand and appreciate your evidence-based argument—and think about the case you have made for it

Your final writing assignment—the development of an evidence-based argumentative essay—will provide you with opportunities to use all of these related skills and to demonstrate your proficiency and growth in building evidence-based arguments. The assignment will also represent your final work in the Core Proficiencies sequence and should demonstrate all that you have learned as a reader, thinker, and writer this year.

FINAL ASSIGNMENT

Developing, Writing, and Revising an Evidence-Based Argumentative Essay: Having read a collection of informational texts and arguments related to the unit's issue, you will develop a supported position on the issue. You will then plan, draft, and revise a multiparagraph essay that makes a case for your position. To do this, you will do the following:

1. Review the texts you have read, the tools you have completed, and the claims you have formed throughout the unit to determine the position you will take on the issue.
2. Write a paragraph that clearly states and explains your position—and the support you have found for it.
3. Read or reread arguments related to your position, looking for evidence you might use to support your argument.
4. Use a **Delineating Arguments Tool** to plan a multiparagraph essay that presents a series of claims, supported by evidence, to develop an argument in favor of your position.
5. Draft a multiparagraph essay that explains, develops, and supports your argumentative position—keeping in mind these criteria for this final writing assignment. Your essay should accomplish the following:

- Present a convincing argument that comes from your understanding of the issue and a clear perspective and position.
- Organize a set of claims in an order that explains and supports your position.
- Use relevant and trustworthy evidence to support all claims and your overall position.
- Represent the best thinking and writing you can do.

FINAL WRITING TASK (Continued)

FINAL ASSIGNMENT

6. Use a collaborative process with other students to review and improve your draft in key areas:

- The information and ideas that make up your argument
- The organization (unity and logical sequence) of your argument
- Your selection, use, and integration of supporting evidence (e.g., quotations, facts, statistics, references to other arguments)
- The clarity of your writing—in areas identified by your teacher

7. Reflect on how well you have used literacy skills and academic habits throughout the unit and in developing your final written argument.

SKILLS AND HABITS TO BE DEMONSTRATED

As you become an expert on your issue and develop your evidence-based position and argument, think about demonstrating the literacy skills and academic habits listed in the following areas to the best of your ability. Your teacher will evaluate your work and determine your grade based on how well you demonstrate these skills and habits.

Read

Recognize perspective: Identify and explain each author's view of the unit's issue.

Evaluate information: Assess the relevance and credibility of information in texts about the issue.

Delineate arguments: Identify and analyze the claims, evidence, and reasoning of arguments related to the issue.

Develop Academic Habits

Remain open to new ideas: Ask questions of others rather than arguing for your own ideas or opinions.

Qualify your views: Explain and change your ideas in response to thinking from others.

Revise: Rethink your position and refine your writing based on feedback from others.

Reflect critically: Discuss and evaluate your learning, using the criteria that describe the literacy skills and academic habits you have been developing.

Write

Form claims: State meaningful positions and conclusions that are well supported by evidence from texts you have examined.

Use evidence: Use well-chosen details from the texts to support your position and claims. Accurately paraphrase or quote what the authors say in the texts.

Use logic: Argue for your position through a logical sequence of related claims, premises, and supporting evidence.

FINAL WRITING TASK (Continued)

ODELL
EDUCATION

TEXT 1.1 — *WHAT IS A PERFORMANCE-ENHANCING DRUG?*

Luke Bauer

Odell Education, December 5, 2013

Performance-enhancing drugs (PEDS) are taken by athletes to increase their abilities or performance in a sport. The term *performance-enhancing drugs* refers to a variety of substances used by athletes. This list includes anabolic steroids and human growth hormone. PEDS are often used to build strong muscles and recover from injuries. Many athletic leagues have rules that do not allow athletes to use PEDS.

There is evidence of PEDS being used thousands of years ago. The Greeks created performance drinks to increase their abilities. The Mayans used cocoa leaves to increase their abilities. Today, athletes will go to many lengths to increase athletic ability.

Most young athletes will tell you that there is a lot of pressure to win. Besides the satisfaction of personal gain, young athletes often pursue dreams of making it to the Olympics, a college scholarship or a place on a professional team. In this environment, using PEDS often seems a good way to stay competitive.

For a growing number of athletes, winning at all costs leads to using PEDS. Some may appear to achieve physical gains from such drugs, but at what cost? Are there health dangers to using PEDS? The truth is that long-term effects of steroids and other performance-enhancing drugs haven't been rigorously studied.

UNDERSTANDING THE NATURE OF AN ISSUE

OVERVIEW AND TOOLS

"The use of enhancement 'substances' for sporting events dates back to the ancient Greeks and ancient Maya."

OBJECTIVE:	To apply your close-reading skills to understand a complex societal issue.

MATERIALS:
- *Guiding Questions Handout*
- *Questioning Path Tool*
- *Forming EBC Tool*

TEXTS

Text Set 1: Background Informational Texts
- 1.1 *"What Is a Performance-Enhancing Drug?"*
- 1.2 *"Historical Timeline: History of Performance Enhancing Drugs in Sports*
- 1.3 *"Steroids"*

- *Organizing EBC Tool*
- *EBA Terms*

Text Set 2: Additional Background Informational Texts
- 2.1 *"How to Get Doping out of Sports"*
- 2.2 *"Performance Enhancing Drugs Outside of Pro Sports"*
- 2.3 *"Performance Enhancing Drugs: A Cheat Sheet"*

⟱ ACTIVITIES

1. INTRODUCING THE UNIT
Your teacher presents an overview of the unit and its societal issue.

2. EXPLORING THE ISSUE
You read and analyze a background text to develop an initial understanding of the issue.

3. DEEPENING UNDERSTANDING OF THE ISSUE
You read and analyze an additional background text to deepen your understanding of the issue.

4. QUESTIONING TO REFINE UNDERSTANDING
You develop text-dependent questions to guide your reading and expand your knowledge of the issue.

5. WRITING AN EBC ABOUT THE NATURE OF THE ISSUE
You write a multipart evidence-based claim about the nature of the issue.

QUESTIONING PATH TOOL

Text 1.1—"What Is a Performance Enhancing Drug?"

APPROACHING: *I determine my reading purposes and take note of key information about the text. I identify the LIPS domain(s) that will guide my initial reading.*

QUESTIONING: *I use Guiding Questions to help me investigate the text (from the Guiding Questions Handout).*

ANALYZING: *I question further to connect and analyze the details I find (from the Guiding Questions Handout).*

1. What do I think the text is mainly about—what is discussed in detail?

2. How might I summarize the main ideas of the text and the key supporting details?

DEEPENING: *I consider the questions of others.*

3. How does the author define performance-enhancing drugs? What words are used?

4. What comparison is made between modern athletes and ancient Greek and Mayan athletes?

5. What does the author suggest as key reasons why athletes may decide to use PEDs?

EXTENDING: *I pose my own questions.*

What evidence does this text provide that builds my understanding of the issue of performance-enhancing drugs?

QUESTIONING PATH TOOL

Text 1.2—Historical Timeline: History of Performance Enhancing Drugs in Sports

APPROACHING:
I determine my reading purposes and take note of key information about the text. I identify the LIPS domain(s) that will guide my initial reading.

QUESTIONING: *I use Guiding Questions to help me investigate the text (from the **Guiding Questions Handout**).*

ANALYZING: *I question further to connect and analyze the details I find (from the **Guiding Questions Handout**).*

1. What do I notice about how the text is organized or sequenced?

2. What unfamiliar words do I need to study or define to better understand the text?

DEEPENING: *I consider the questions of others.*

3. In any year or era, what does the time line's text say happened regarding the use of performance-enhancing drugs?

4. In that year or era, what does the time line suggest about the impacts of PEDs on athletes and athletic competitions?

5. In that year or era, what does the time line suggest about how society and people who care about sports responded to the use of PEDs?

EXTENDING: *I pose my own questions.*

What evidence does this text provide that builds my understanding of the issue of performance-enhancing drugs?

ODELL
EDUCATION

QUESTIONING PATH TOOL

Text 1.3—"Steroids"

APPROACHING:
I determine my reading purposes and take note of key information about the text. I identify the LIPS domain(s) that will guide my initial reading.

QUESTIONING: *I use Guiding Questions to help me investigate the text (from the **Guiding Questions Handout**).*

ANALYZING: *I question further to connect and analyze the details I find (from the **Guiding Questions Handout**).*

1. What unfamiliar words do I need to study or define to better understand the text?

2. What claims do I find in the text?

3. What evidence supports the claims in the text, and what is left uncertain or unsupported?

DEEPENING: *I consider the questions of others.*

4. What are steroids and how do they work?

5. What does the article say about the dangers of using steroids?

6. The article concludes with the claim that "using steroids is cheating." Does the article present evidence to support this claim, and if so, what is the evidence?

EXTENDING: *I pose my own questions.*

What evidence does this text provide that builds my understanding of the issue of performance-enhancing drugs?

ANALYZING DETAILS TOOL

Name _ _ _ _ _ _ _ _ _ _ _ _ _ _ _ _ _ _ _ Text _ _ _ _ _ _ _ _ _ _ _ _ _ _ _ _ _ _

Reading purpose:

A question I have about the text:

SEARCHING FOR DETAILS

I read the text closely and mark words and phrases that help me think about my question.

SELECTING DETAILS

I select words or phrases from my search that I think are the most important in thinking about my question.

Detail 1 (Ref.:)	Detail 2 (Ref.:)	Detail 3 (Ref.:)

ANALYZING DETAILS

I reread parts of the text and think about the meaning of the <u>details</u> and what they tell me about my question.

What I think about detail 1:	What I think about detail 2:	What I think about detail 3:

CONNECTING DETAILS

I compare the details and explain the <u>connections</u> I see among them.

How I connect the details:

FORMING EVIDENCE-BASED CLAIMS TOOL (EBA)

Name _____   Text _____

A question I have about the text:

_____

SEARCHING FOR DETAILS   I read the text closely and mark words and phrases that help me answer my question.

SELECTING DETAILS	Detail 1 (Ref.:)	Detail 2 (Ref.:)	Detail 3 (Ref.:)
I select words or phrases from my search that I think are the <u>most</u> important for answering my question. I write the reference next to each detail.			

ANALYZING DETAILS

ANALYZING DETAILS	What I think about detail 1:	What I think about detail 2:	What I think about detail 3:
I reread parts of the texts and think about the meaning of the <u>details</u> and what they tell me about my question. Then I compare the details and explain <u>the connections</u> I see among them.			

CONNECTING DETAILS

CONNECTING DETAILS	How I connect the details:
I compare the details and explain <u>the connections</u> I see among them.	

MAKING A CLAIM

MAKING A CLAIM	My claim about the text:
I state a conclusion I have come to and can support with evidence from the text after reading it closely.	

ODELL
EDUCATION

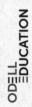

ANALYZING DETAILS TOOL

Name _____

Text _____

Reading purpose:

A question I have about the text:

SEARCHING FOR DETAILS

I read the text closely and mark words and phrases that help me think about my question.

SELECTING DETAILS

I select words or phrases from my search that I think are the most important in thinking about my question.

Detail 1 (Ref.:)	Detail 2 (Ref.:)	Detail 3 (Ref.:)

ANALYZING DETAILS

I reread parts of the text and think about the meaning of the details and what they tell me about my question.

What I think about detail 1:	What I think about detail 2:	What I think about detail 3:

CONNECTING DETAILS

I compare the details and explain the connections I see among them.

How I connect the details:

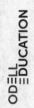

FORMING EVIDENCE-BASED CLAIMS TOOL (EBA)

Name _____   Text _____

A question I have about the text:

SEARCHING FOR DETAILS | I read the text closely and mark words and phrases that help me answer my question.

Detail 1 (Ref.:)	Detail 2 (Ref.:)	Detail 3 (Ref.:)

SELECTING DETAILS

I select words or phrases from my search that I think are the most important for answering my question. I write the reference next to each detail.

ANALYZING DETAILS

What I think about detail 1:	What I think about detail 2:	What I think about detail 3:

I reread parts of the texts and think about the meaning of the details and what they tell me about my question. Then I compare the details and explain the connections I see among them.

CONNECTING DETAILS

How I connect the details:

I compare the details and explain the connections I see among them.

MAKING A CLAIM

My claim about the text:

I state a conclusion I have come to and can support with evidence from the text after reading it closely.

ODELL
EDUCATION

QUESTIONING PATH TOOL

Text 2.1—"How to Get Doping out of Sports"

APPROACHING: *I determine my reading purposes and take note of key information about the text. I identify the LIPS domain(s) that will guide my initial reading.*	
QUESTIONING: *I use Guiding Questions to help me investigate the text (from the **Guiding Questions Handout**).*	
ANALYZING: *I question further to connect and analyze the details I find (from the **Guiding Questions Handout**).*	1. What do I think the text is mainly about—what is discussed in detail? 2. What claims do I find in the text? 3. How might I summarize the main ideas of the text and the key supporting details?
DEEPENING: *I consider the questions of others.*	4. What are the details of the author's own story as a young athlete? What does his story suggest about why some athletes decide to use PEDs? 5. What is the "2%" that Vaughters describes? Why is it so important in sports? 6. What connection does Vaughters make between the 2% and doping? 7. What textual details support Vaughters claim that "achieving childhood dreams is a hard road"? 8. What does Vaughters mean in paragraph 9 when he says, "The answer is not to teach young athletes that giving up lifelong dreams is better than giving in to cheating. The answer is to never give them the option"?
EXTENDING: *I pose my own questions.*	What evidence does this text provide that builds my understanding of the issue of performance-enhancing drugs?

ODELL
EDUCATION

QUESTIONING PATH TOOL

Text 2.2—"Performance-Enhancing Drugs outside of Pro Sports"

APPROACHING: *I determine my reading purposes and take note of key information about the text. I identify the LIPS domain(s) that will guide my initial reading.*

QUESTIONING: *I use Guiding Questions to help me investigate the text (from the **Guiding Questions Handout**).*

ANALYZING: *I question further to connect and analyze the details I find (from the **Guiding Questions Handout**).*

1. What do I think the text is mainly about—what is discussed in detail?

2. What claims do I find in the text?

3. How might I summarize the main ideas of the text and the key supporting details?

DEEPENING: *I consider the questions of others.*

4. Dr. Jeffrey Life states, early in the video, "I'm not against aging. I'm against getting old." What is his position about the use of steroids and human growth hormone? What evidence does the video provide for his view?

5. What are the potential long-terms health effects of using human growth hormone that are identified by Dr. Tom Perls from Boston University?

EXTENDING: *I pose my own questions.*

What evidence does this text provide that builds my understanding of the issue of the use of performance-enhancing drugs?

QUESTIONING PATH TOOL

Text 2.3—"Performance-Enhancing Drugs: A Cheat Sheet"

APPROACHING: *I determine my reading purposes and take note of key information about the text. I identify the LIPS domain(s) that will guide my initial reading.*

QUESTIONING: *I use Guiding Questions to help me investigate the text (from the **Guiding Questions Handout**).*

ANALYZING: *I question further to connect and analyze the details I find (from the **Guiding Questions Handout**).*

1. What do I think the text is mainly about—what is discussed in detail?

2. What claims do I find in the text?

3. How might I summarize the main ideas of the text and the key supporting details?

DEEPENING: *I consider the questions of others.*

4. For any of the drugs detailed in the sections of this article, how do they work, what are the health risks, and how often are they used by athletes?

EXTENDING: *I pose my own questions.*

What evidence does this text provide that builds my understanding of the issue of the use of performance-enhancing drugs

ODELL EDUCATION

FORMING EVIDENCE-BASED CLAIMS TOOL (EBA)

Name _____

Text _____

A question I have about the text:

_____

SEARCHING FOR DETAILS

I read the text closely and mark words and phrases that help me answer my question.

Detail 1 (Ref.:)	Detail 2 (Ref.:)	Detail 3 (Ref.:)

SELECTING DETAILS

I select words or phrases from my search that I think are the most important for answering my question. I write the reference next to each detail.

ANALYZING DETAILS

I reread parts of the texts and think about the meaning of the details and what they tell me about my question. Then I compare the details and explain the connections I see among them.

What I think about detail 1:	What I think about detail 2:	What I think about detail 3:

CONNECTING DETAILS

I compare the details and explain the connections I see among them.

How I connect the details:

MAKING A CLAIM

I state a conclusion I have come to and can support with evidence from the text after reading it closely.

My claim about the text:

ODELL
EDUCATION

FORMING EVIDENCE-BASED CLAIMS TOOL (EBA)

Name ------------------------------------ **Text** ------------------------------------

A question I have about the text:

SEARCHING FOR DETAILS

I read the text closely and mark words and phrases that help me answer my question.

SELECTING DETAILS

I select words or phrases from my search that I think are the most important for answering my question. I write the reference next to each detail.

| Detail 1 (Ref.:) | Detail 2 (Ref.:) | Detail 3 (Ref.:) |

ANALYZING DETAILS

I reread parts of the texts and think about the meaning of the details and what they tell me about my question. Then I compare the details and explain the connections I see among them.

| What I think about detail 1: | What I think about detail 2: | What I think about detail 3: |

CONNECTING DETAILS

I compare the details and explain the connections I see among them.

How I connect the details:

MAKING A CLAIM

I state a conclusion I have come to and can support with evidence from the text after reading it closely.

My claim about the text:

FORMING EVIDENCE-BASED CLAIMS TOOL (EBA)

Name _____   Text _____

A question I have about the text:

SEARCHING FOR DETAILS

I read the text closely and mark words and phrases that help me answer my question.

SELECTING DETAILS

I select words or phrases from my search that I think are the most important for answering my question. I write the reference next to each detail.

Detail 1 (Ref.:)	Detail 2 (Ref.:)	Detail 3 (Ref.:)

ANALYZING DETAILS

I reread parts of the texts and think about the meaning of the details and what they tell me about my question. Then I compare the details and explain the connections I see among them.

What I think about detail 1:	What I think about detail 2:	What I think about detail 3:

CONNECTING DETAILS

I compare the details and explain the connections I see among them.

How I connect the details:

MAKING A CLAIM

I state a conclusion I have come to and can support with evidence from the text after reading it closely.

My claim about the text:

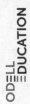

ODELL
EDUCATION

QUESTIONING PATH TOOL

Name: _____ **Text:** _____

APPROACHING: *I determine my reading purposes and take note of key information about the text. I identify the LIPS domain(s) that will guide my initial reading.*	Purpose: Key information: LIPS domain(s):
QUESTIONING: *I use Guiding Questions to help me investigate the text (from the **Guiding Questions Handout**).*	1. 2.
ANALYZING: *I question further to connect and analyze the details I find (from the **Guiding Questions Handout**).*	1. 2.
DEEPENING: *I consider the questions of others.*	1. 2. 3.
EXTENDING: *I pose my own questions.*	1. 2.

ODELL EDUCATION

QUESTIONING PATH TOOL

Name: _____ **Text:** _____

APPROACHING: *I determine my reading purposes and take note of key information about the text. I identify the LIPS domain(s) that will guide my initial reading.*

Purpose:

Key information:

LIPS domain(s):

QUESTIONING: *I use Guiding Questions to help me investigate the text (from the **Guiding Questions Handout**).*

1.

2.

ANALYZING: *I question further to connect and analyze the details I find (from the **Guiding Questions Handout**).*

1.

2.

DEEPENING: *I consider the questions of others.*

1.

2.

3.

EXTENDING: *I pose my own questions.*

1.

2.

ORGANIZING EVIDENCE-BASED CLAIMS TOOL (2 POINTS)

Name _ _ _ _ _ _ _ _ _ _   Text _

CLAIM:

Point 1

Point 2

A Supporting Evidence	**B** Supporting Evidence	**A** Supporting Evidence
(Reference:)	(Reference:)	(Reference:)
C Supporting Evidence	**D** Supporting Evidence	**C** Supporting Evidence
(Reference:)	(Reference:)	(Reference:)

B Supporting Evidence

(Reference:)

D Supporting Evidence

(Reference:)

ODELL
EDUCATION

ORGANIZING EVIDENCE-BASED CLAIMS TOOL (3 POINTS)

Name _ _ _ _ _ _ _ _ _ Text _ _ _ _ _ _ _ _ _

CLAIM:

Point 1	Point 2	Point 3
A Supporting Evidence	**A** Supporting Evidence	**A** Supporting Evidence
(Reference:)	(Reference:)	(Reference:)
B Supporting Evidence	**B** Supporting Evidence	**B** Supporting Evidence
(Reference:)	(Reference:)	(Reference:)
C Supporting Evidence	**C** Supporting Evidence	**C** Supporting Evidence
(Reference:)	(Reference:)	(Reference:)

ORGANIZING EVIDENCE-BASED CLAIMS TOOL (2 POINTS)

Name _ _ _ _ _ _ _ _ _ _ _ Text _ _ _ _ _ _ _ _ _ _ _

CLAIM:

Point 1

A Supporting Evidence	**B** Supporting Evidence
(Reference:)	(Reference:)
C Supporting Evidence	**D** Supporting Evidence
(Reference:)	(Reference:)

Point 2

A Supporting Evidence	**B** Supporting Evidence
(Reference:)	(Reference:)
C Supporting Evidence	**D** Supporting Evidence
(Reference:)	(Reference:)

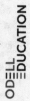

ORGANIZING EVIDENCE-BASED CLAIMS TOOL (3 POINTS)

Name _ _ _ _ _ _ _ _ _ _ _ Text _ _ _ _ _ _ _ _ _ _ _

CLAIM:

	Point 1	Point 2	Point 3
A	Supporting Evidence	Supporting Evidence	Supporting Evidence
	(Reference:)	(Reference:)	(Reference:)
B	Supporting Evidence	Supporting Evidence	Supporting Evidence
	(Reference:)	(Reference:)	(Reference:)
C	Supporting Evidence	Supporting Evidence	Supporting Evidence
	(Reference:)	(Reference:)	(Reference:)

PART 2

ANALYZING ARGUMENTS

OVERVIEW AND TOOLS

"The drugs are illegal, they're harmful, and they're cheating."

OBJECTIVE:	To delineate and analyze different parts of arguments.

MATERIALS:
- *Guiding Questions Handout*
- *Forming EBC Tool*

TEXTS
- *3 Cartoonists on Baseball and Steroids*

Text Set 4: Seminal Arguments
- *4.1 Congressman Elijah E. Cummings Urges the National Basketball Association to Adopt a Zero-Tolerance Drug Policy*
- *4.2 Speech by Dr. Jacques Rogge, president, International Olympic Committee to World Conference on Doping in Sport*
- *4.3 "Why It's Time to Legalize Steroids in Professional Sports"*
- *4.4 "Confessions of a Doper: Lance Armstrong's Former Teammate Jonathan Vaughters Talks about Why Some Athletes Use Steroids."*

- *Delineating Arguments Tool*
- *Model Arguments*

Text Set 5: Additional Arguments
- *5.1 "No Place In High School Sports for Performance-Enhancing Drugs"*
- *5.2 "Did Lance Armstrong Cheat? I Don't Care"*
- *5.3 "Lance Armstrong Had Little Choice but to Dope"*
- *5.4 "There Are No Sound Moral Arguments Against Performance-Enhancing Drugs"*

☰ ACTIVITIES

1. UNDERSTANDING ARGUMENTATIVE POSITION
Your teacher uses the unit's issue to discuss what an argumentative position is.

2. IDENTIFYING ELEMENTS OF ARGUMENTATION
Your teacher introduces and the class explores the different parts of argumentation using model arguments.

3. DELINEATING ARGUMENTATION
In teams, you read and delineate arguments and write an evidence-based claim about one author's argument.

ODELL
EDUCATION

4. UNDERSTANDING PERSPECTIVE
Your teacher discusses what perspective is and how it relates to argumentation.

5. COMPARING PERSPECTIVES
You analyze and compare perspectives in argumentative texts.

6. DELINEATING ADDITIONAL ARGUMENTS
As needed, you read and analyze more arguments related to the unit's issue.

7. WRITING TO ANALYZE ARGUMENTS
Write short essays analyzing an argument.

QUESTIONING PATH TOOL

Name: _____ **Text:** _____

APPROACHING: *I determine my reading purposes and take note of key information about the text. I identify the LIPS domain(s) that will guide my initial reading.*

Purpose:

Key information:

LIPS domain(s):

QUESTIONING: *I use Guiding Questions to help me investigate the text (from the **Guiding Questions Handout**).*

1.

2.

ANALYZING: *I question further to connect and analyze the details I find (from the **Guiding Questions Handout**).*

1.

2.

DEEPENING: *I consider the questions of others.*

1.

2.

3.

EXTENDING: *I pose my own questions.*

1.

2.

ODELL EDUCATION

QUESTIONING PATH TOOL

Name: _____ Text: _____

APPROACHING: *I determine my reading purposes and take note of key information about the text. I identify the LIPS domain(s) that will guide my initial reading.*	Purpose: Key information: LIPS domain(s):
QUESTIONING: *I use Guiding Questions to help me investigate the text (from the* ***Guiding Questions Handout***).	1. 2.
ANALYZING: *I question further to connect and analyze the details I find (from the* ***Guiding Questions Handout***).	1. 2.
DEEPENING: *I consider the questions of others.*	1. 2. 3.
EXTENDING: *I pose my own questions.*	1. 2.

DELINEATING ARGUMENTS TOOL

Name _ _ _ _ _ _ _ _ _ _ _ _ _ _ **Topic** _ _ _ _ _ _ _ _ _ _ _ _

ISSUE

PERSPECTIVE

POSITION

PREMISE/CLAIM 1
Supporting evidence:

PREMISE/CLAIM 2
Supporting evidence:

PREMISE/CLAIM 3
Supporting evidence:

ODELL EDUCATION

QUESTIONING PATH TOOL

Text 4.1—Congressman Elijah E. Cummings Urges the National Basketball Association to Adopt a Zero-Tolerance Drug Policy

APPROACHING: *I determine my reading purposes and take note of key information about the text. I identify the LIPS domain(s) that will guide my initial reading.*

QUESTIONING: *I use Guiding Questions to help me investigate the text (from the **Guiding Questions Handout**).*

ANALYZING: *I question further to connect and analyze the details I find (from the **Guiding Questions Handout**).*

1. What do I think the text is mainly about—what is discussed in detail?

2. What claims do I find in the text?

3. How might I summarize the main ideas of the text and the key supporting details?

DEEPENING: *I consider the questions of others.*

4. What does the first line of Cummings's release ("... steroid abuse in professional sports is no game") imply about his position on performance-enhancing drugs?

5. What information is given in the article to indicate Cummings's perspective on the issue of PEDs?

6. What evidence does Cummings use to support his claim that youth are receiving "destructive messages" about performance-enhancing drugs?

7. Which sentences—taken together—best communicate Cummings's position about performance-enhancing drugs in sports?

EXTENDING: *I pose my own questions.*

What evidence does this text provide that builds my understanding of the issue of performance-enhancing drugs?

QUESTIONING PATH TOOL

Text 4.2—Speech by Dr. Jacques Rogge, President, International Olympic Committee to World Conference on Doping in Sport

APPROACHING: *I determine my reading purposes and take note of key information about the text. I identify the LIPS domain(s) that will guide my initial reading.*

QUESTIONING: *I use Guiding Questions to help me investigate the text (from the Guiding Questions Handout).*

ANALYZING: *I question further to connect and analyze the details I find (from the Guiding Questions Handout).*

1. How does the author's choice of words reveal his or her purposes and perspective?

2. How does the author's perspective influence his or her presentation of ideas, themes, or arguments?

3. What claims do I find in the text?

DEEPENING: *I consider the questions of others.*

4. What does the section "The importance of our efforts" reveal about Rogge's position on doping? What does this section tell you about his perspective on doping?

5. In building support for his argument, Rogge claims that "the fight against doping involves however much more than elite sport alone." What other groups does Rogge mention as support for his claim?

6. What "further challenges" in the fight against doping in sport does Rogge identify? What might the implications of these challenges be?

7. How does Rogge's position and perspective on doping compare to that of Cummings (Text 4.1)?

EXTENDING: *I pose my own questions.*

What evidence does this text provide that builds my understanding of various perspectives on the issue of performance-enhancing drugs?

ODELL EDUCATION

QUESTIONING PATH TOOL

Text 4.3—"Why It's Time To Legalize Steroids in Professional Sports"

APPROACHING:
I determine my reading purposes and take note of key information about the text. I identify the LIPS domain(s) that will guide my initial reading.

QUESTIONING: *I use Guiding Questions to help me investigate the text (from the **Guiding Questions Handout**).*

ANALYZING: *I question further to connect and analyze the details I find (from the **Guiding Questions Handout**).*

1. How does the author's choice of words reveal his or her purposes and perspective?

2. How does the author's perspective influence his or her presentation of ideas, themes, or arguments?

3. What claims do I find in the text?

DEEPENING: *I consider the questions of others.*

4. What is Smith's perspective on the problem of performance-enhancing drugs in sports? How does Smith's language show his perspective?

5. Although Smith makes a number of claims in his argument, some are supported and some are not. Which claims does he support with evidence and which does he not?

6. Which details and evidence that Smith cites seem solid and convincing? Which ones seem more questionable or in need of more evidence?

7. Smith says, "The primary reason why performance-enhancing drugs (PEDs) are outlawed in professional sports is that [they] give users an unfair advantages over the rest of the field." How does this claim compare with ideas presented by Cummings (Text 4.1) and Rogge (Text 4.2)?

EXTENDING: *I pose my own questions.*

What evidence does this text provide that builds my understanding of various perspectives on the issue of performance-enhancing drugs?

DELINEATING ARGUMENTS TOOL

Name _ _ _ _ _ _ _ _ _ _ _ _ _ _ _ Topic _

ISSUE	

PERSPECTIVE	

POSITION	

PREMISE/CLAIM 1	
	Supporting evidence:

PREMISE/CLAIM 2	
	Supporting evidence:

PREMISE/CLAIM 3	
	Supporting evidence:

ODELL EDUCATION

ORGANIZING EVIDENCE-BASED CLAIMS TOOL (2 POINTS)

Name _ _ _ _ _ _ _ _ _ _ _ _ _

Text _ _ _ _ _ _ _ _ _ _ _ _ _

CLAIM:

Point 1

A Supporting Evidence	**B** Supporting Evidence
(Reference:)	(Reference:)
C Supporting Evidence	**D** Supporting Evidence
(Reference:)	(Reference:)

Point 2

A Supporting Evidence	**B** Supporting Evidence
(Reference:)	(Reference:)
C Supporting Evidence	**D** Supporting Evidence
(Reference:)	(Reference:)

ODELL EDUCATION

ORGANIZING EVIDENCE-BASED CLAIMS TOOL (3 POINTS)

Name _ _ _ _ _ _ _ _ _ _ _ _ _ _   Text _ _ _ _ _ _ _ _ _ _ _

CLAIM:

Point 1	Point 2	Point 3
A Supporting Evidence	**A** Supporting Evidence	**A** Supporting Evidence
(Reference:)	(Reference:)	(Reference:)
B Supporting Evidence	**B** Supporting Evidence	**B** Supporting Evidence
(Reference:)	(Reference:)	(Reference:)
C Supporting Evidence	**C** Supporting Evidence	**C** Supporting Evidence
(Reference:)	(Reference:)	(Reference:)

PART 3

EVALUATING ARGUMENTS AND DEVELOPING A POSITION

OVERVIEW AND TOOLS

"At their best, sports can embody the virtues of teamwork, hard work, and integrity"

OBJECTIVE:	To evaluate arguments, determine which arguments you find most convincing, and synthesize what you have learned so far to establish your own position.

MATERIALS:
- *Forming EBC Tool*
- *Delineating Arguments Tool*
- *Evaluating Arguments Tool*
- *Organizing EBC Tool*
- *Student EBA Literacy Skills and Academic Habits Checklist*
- *EBA Terms*

TEXT SET
- *3 Cartoonists on Baseball and Steroids*

Text Set 4: Seminal Arguments
- *4.1 Congressman Elijah E. Cummings Urges the National Basketball Association to Adopt a Zero-Tolerance Drug Policy*
- *4.2 Speech by Dr. Jacques Rogge, president, International Olympic Committee to World Conference on Doping in Sport*
- *4.3 "Why It's Time to Legalize Steroids in Professional Sports"*
- *4.4 "Confessions of a Doper: Lance Armstrong's Former Teammate Jonathan Vaughters Talks about Why Some Athletes Use Steroids."*

Text Set 5: Additional Arguments
- *5.1 "No Place In High School Sports for Performance-Enhancing Drugs"*
- *5.2 "Did Lance Armstrong Cheat? I Don't Care"*
- *5.3 "Lance Armstrong Had Little Choice but to Dope"*
- *5.4 "There Are No Sound Moral Arguments Against Performance-Enhancing Drugs"*

≡ ACTIVITIES

1. EVALUATING ARGUMENTS
You review and evaluate arguments based on your own developing perspective on the issue.

2. DEVELOPING A POSITION
You synthesize what you have learned about the issue and arguments, and work on developing your perspective and position on the issue.

3. DEEPENING UNDERSTANDING

If needed, you research more to help develop and support your position.

4. USING OTHERS' ARGUMENTS TO SUPPORT A POSITION

You identify an argument that supports your position and write an evidence-based claim about why the argument is convincing or makes sense to you.

5. RESPONDING TO OPPOSING ARGUMENTS

You identify an argument that is against your position and write an evidence-based claim that:

- recognizes the argument's position
- points out its limitations
- refutes its claims
- or refutes it as invalid, illogical, or unsupported.

ODELL
EDUCATION

EVALUATING ARGUMENTS TOOL

As you read and delineate the argument, think about each of the **elements** and their **guiding evaluation questions.** Rate each element as:

? a **questionable** part or weakness of the argument   ✔ a reasonable or **acceptable** part of the argument   **+** a **strength** of the argument

ELEMENTS	EVALUATING AN ARGUMENT: GUIDING QUESTIONS	?	✔	+	TEXT-BASED OBSERVATIONS
Issue	• How clearly is the issue presented and explained? • How accurate and current is the explanation of the issue?				
Perspective	• What is the author's relationship to the issue? What is the author's purpose for the argument? • What are the author's background and credentials relative to the issue? • What is the author's viewpoint or attitude about the issue? How reasonable is this perspective?				
Position	• How clearly is the author's position presented and explained? • How well is the position connected to the claims and evidence of the argument?				
Claims	• How clearly are the argument's claims explained and connected to the position? • Are the claims supported with evidence? • How well are the claims linked together into an argument?				
Evidence	• Does the supporting evidence come from a trustworthy source? Is it believable? • Is there enough evidence to make the argument convincing?				
Conclusions	• How logical and reasonable are the conclusions drawn by the author? • How well do the argument's conclusions or suggestions address the issue and align with the position?				
Convincing Argument	• How do the author's overall perspective and position on the issue compare with others? With my own? • Does the argument make sense to me? Do I agree with its claims? Am I convinced?				
Comments:					

EVALUATING ARGUMENTS TOOL

As you read and delineate the argument, think about each of the **elements** and their **guiding evaluation questions**. Rate each element as:

? a **questionable** part or weakness of the argument ✔ a reasonable or **acceptable** part of the argument **+** a **strength** of the argument

ELEMENTS	EVALUATING AN ARGUMENT: GUIDING QUESTIONS	?	✔	+	TEXT-BASED OBSERVATIONS
Issue	• How clearly is the issue presented and explained? • How accurate and current is the explanation of the issue?				
Perspective	• What is the author's relationship to the issue? What is the author's purpose for the argument? • What are the author's background and credentials relative to the issue? • What is the author's viewpoint or attitude about the issue? How reasonable is this perspective?				
Position	• How clearly is the author's position presented and explained? • How well is the position connected to the claims and evidence of the argument?				
Claims	• How clearly are the argument's claims explained and connected to the position? • Are the claims supported with evidence? • How well are the claims linked together into an argument?				
Evidence	• Does the supporting evidence come from a trustworthy source? Is it believable? • Is there enough evidence to make the argument convincing?				
Conclusions	• How logical and reasonable are the conclusions drawn by the author? • How well do the argument's conclusions or suggestions address the issue and align with the position?				
Convincing Argument	• How do the author's overall perspective and position on the issue compare with others? With my own? • Does the argument make sense to me? Do I agree with its claims? Am I convinced?				
Comments:					

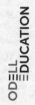

ODELL
EDUCATION

EVALUATING ARGUMENTS TOOL

As you read and delineate the argument, think about each of the **elements** and their **guiding evaluation questions.** Rate each element as:

? a **questionable** part or weakness of the argument   ✔ a reasonable or **acceptable** part of the argument   **+** a **strength** of the argument

ELEMENTS	EVALUATING AN ARGUMENT: GUIDING QUESTIONS	?	✔	+	TEXT-BASED OBSERVATIONS
Issue	• How clearly is the issue presented and explained? • How accurate and current is the explanation of the issue?				
Perspective	• What is the author's relationship to the issue? What is the author's purpose for the argument? • What are the author's background and credentials relative to the issue? • What is the author's viewpoint or attitude about the issue? How reasonable is this perspective?				
Position	• How clearly is the author's position presented and explained? • How well is the position connected to the claims and evidence of the argument?				
Claims	• How clearly are the argument's claims explained and connected to the position? • Are the claims supported with evidence? • How well are the claims linked together into an argument?				
Evidence	• Does the supporting evidence come from a trustworthy source? Is it believable? • Is there enough evidence to make the argument convincing?				
Conclusions	• How logical and reasonable are the conclusions drawn by the author? • How well do the argument's conclusions or suggestions address the issue and align with the position?				
Convincing Argument	• How do the author's overall perspective and position on the issue compare with others? With my own? • Does the argument make sense to me? Do I agree with its claims? Am I convinced?				
Comments:					

ORGANIZING EVIDENCE-BASED CLAIMS TOOL (2 POINTS)

Name _____   Text _____

CLAIM:

Point 1

A Supporting Evidence

(Reference:)

B Supporting Evidence

(Reference:)

C Supporting Evidence

(Reference:)

D Supporting Evidence

(Reference:)

Point 2

A Supporting Evidence

(Reference:)

B Supporting Evidence

(Reference:)

C Supporting Evidence

(Reference:)

D Supporting Evidence

(Reference:)

ODELL EDUCATION

ORGANIZING EVIDENCE-BASED CLAIMS TOOL (3 POINTS)

Name _ _ _ _ _ _ _ _ _ _ _ _ _ _ _ _ _ _ Text _ _ _ _ _ _ _ _ _ _ _ _ _ _ _ _ _

CLAIM:

Point 1	Point 2	Point 3
A Supporting Evidence	**A** Supporting Evidence	**A** Supporting Evidence
(Reference:)	(Reference:)	(Reference:)
B Supporting Evidence	**B** Supporting Evidence	**B** Supporting Evidence
(Reference:)	(Reference:)	(Reference:)
C Supporting Evidence	**C** Supporting Evidence	**C** Supporting Evidence
(Reference:)	(Reference:)	(Reference:)

ODELL
EDUCATION

DELINEATING ARGUMENTS TOOL

Name _ _ _ _ _ _ _ _ _ _ Topic _ _ _ _ _ _

ISSUE	

PERSPECTIVE	

POSITION	

PREMISE/CLAIM 1	
Supporting evidence:	

PREMISE/CLAIM 2	
Supporting evidence:	

PREMISE/CLAIM 3	
Supporting evidence:	

ODELL EDUCATION

DELINEATING ARGUMENTS TOOL

Name _____ Topic _____

ISSUE

PERSPECTIVE

POSITION

PREMISE/CLAIM 1	
	Supporting evidence:

PREMISE/CLAIM 2	
	Supporting evidence:

PREMISE/CLAIM 3	
	Supporting evidence:

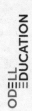
ODELL EDUCATION

EVALUATING ARGUMENTS TOOL

As you read and delineate the argument, think about each of the **elements** and their **guiding evaluation questions**. Rate each element as:

? a **questionable** part or weakness of the argument   ✔ a reasonable or **acceptable** part of the argument   **+** a **strength** of the argument

ELEMENTS	EVALUATING AN ARGUMENT: GUIDING QUESTIONS	?	✔	+	TEXT-BASED OBSERVATIONS
Issue	• How clearly is the issue presented and explained? • How accurate and current is the explanation of the issue?				
Perspective	• What is the author's relationship to the issue? What is the author's purpose for the argument? • What are the author's background and credentials relative to the issue? • What is the author's viewpoint or attitude about the issue? How reasonable is this perspective?				
Position	• How clearly is the author's position presented and explained? • How well is the position connected to the claims and evidence of the argument?				
Claims	• How clearly are the argument's claims explained and connected to the position? • Are the claims supported with evidence? • How well are the claims linked together into an argument?				
Evidence	• Does the supporting evidence come from a trustworthy source? Is it believable? • Is there enough evidence to make the argument convincing?				
Conclusions	• How logical and reasonable are the conclusions drawn by the author? • How well do the argument's conclusions or suggestions address the issue and align with the position?				
Convincing Argument	• How do the author's overall perspective and position on the issue compare with others? With my own? • Does the argument make sense to me? Do I agree with its claims? Am I convinced?				

Comments:

PART 4

ORGANIZING AN
EVIDENCE-BASED ARGUMENT

OVERVIEW AND TOOLS

"This is about more than safeguarding
fair play—it's about saving lives."

OBJECTIVE:	To write premises and sequence them to create a coherent, logical argument.

MATERIALS:
- *Forming EBC Tool*
- *Organizing EBC Tool*
- *Delineating Arguments Tool*
- *EBA Terms*

ACTIVITIES

1. IDENTIFYING SUPPORTING EVIDENCE
Review your notes, tools, and previously written claims to figure out what you will use as evidence to develop and support your position.

2. DEVELOPING AND SEQUENCING CLAIMS AS PREMISES OF THE ARGUMENT
Review the claims you have previously written (and maybe write new claims) to figure out how you will use them as premises to develop your argument. Think of a potential sequence for your premises.

3. ORGANIZING EVIDENCE TO SUPPORT CLAIMS
List and sequence your claims. Then, organize and cite sources for the evidence you will use to explain and support each premise.

4. REVIEWING A PLAN FOR WRITING AN ARGUMENT
Review and revise your plans to make sure that they are clear, strategically sequenced, well-reasoned, and supported by enough evidence.

ORGANIZING EVIDENCE-BASED CLAIMS TOOL (2 POINTS)

Name _

Text _

CLAIM:

Point 1

A   Supporting Evidence

(Reference:)

B   Supporting Evidence

(Reference:)

C   Supporting Evidence

(Reference:)

D   Supporting Evidence

(Reference:)

Point 2

A   Supporting Evidence

(Reference:)

B   Supporting Evidence

(Reference:)

C   Supporting Evidence

(Reference:)

D   Supporting Evidence

(Reference:)

ODELL EDUCATION

ORGANIZING EVIDENCE-BASED CLAIMS TOOL (3 POINTS)

Name _ _ _ _ _ _ _ _ _ _ _ _ _ _ _ _ _ Text _ _ _ _ _ _ _ _ _ _ _ _ _ _ _

CLAIM:

Point 1	Point 2	Point 3
A Supporting Evidence	**A** Supporting Evidence	**A** Supporting Evidence
(Reference:)	(Reference:)	(Reference:)
B Supporting Evidence	**B** Supporting Evidence	**B** Supporting Evidence
(Reference:)	(Reference:)	(Reference:)
C Supporting Evidence	**C** Supporting Evidence	**C** Supporting Evidence
(Reference:)	(Reference:)	(Reference:)

DELINEATING ARGUMENTS TOOL

Name _____ Topic _____

ISSUE	
PERSPECTIVE	
POSITION	

PREMISE/CLAIM 1	PREMISE/CLAIM 2	PREMISE/CLAIM 3
Supporting evidence:	Supporting evidence:	Supporting evidence:

PART 5

DEVELOPING WRITING THROUGH A COLLABORATIVE PROCESS

OVERVIEW AND TOOLS

"For students, writing is a key means of asserting and defending claims, showing what they know about a subject, and conveying what they have experienced, imagined, thought, and felt." CCSS ELA Literacy Standards, p. 41

OBJECTIVE:	To learn and practice how to work with your classmates to improve your writing and write an argumentative essay.

MATERIALS:
- *Student EBA Literacy Skills and Academic Habits Checklist*
- *Connecting Ideas Handout*
- *Organizing EBC Tool*
- *EBA Terms*

ACTIVITIES

1. STRENGTHENING WRITING COLLABORATIVELY: PRINCIPLES AND PROCESSES
Learn and practice how to use criteria and Guiding Questions while working with your classmates to improve your writing and begin drafting your essay.

2. FOCUS ON CONTENT: INFORMATION AND IDEAS
Write, discuss, and revise with a focus on expressing your overall ideas with necessary information.

3. FOCUS ON ORGANIZATION: UNITY, COHERENCE, AND LOGICAL SEQUENCE
Write, discuss, and revise with a focus on the unity, coherence, and logic of your initial draft.

4. FOCUS ON SUPPORT: INTEGRATING AND CITING EVIDENCE
Write, discuss, and revise with a focus on your selection and use of evidence.

5. ADDITIONAL ROUNDS OF FOCUSED REVIEW AND REVISION
Write, discuss, and revise with a focus on additional issues of clarity, grammar, or publication, as determined by your teacher.

ORGANIZING EVIDENCE-BASED CLAIMS TOOL (2 POINTS)

Name _ _ _ _ _ _ _ _ _ _ _ _ _ _ _ **Text** _ _ _ _ _ _ _ _ _ _ _ _ _ _ _

CLAIM:

Point 1

A Supporting Evidence	**B** Supporting Evidence
(Reference:)	(Reference:)
C Supporting Evidence	**D** Supporting Evidence
(Reference:)	(Reference:)

Point 2

A Supporting Evidence	**B** Supporting Evidence
(Reference:)	(Reference:)
C Supporting Evidence	**D** Supporting Evidence
(Reference:)	(Reference:)

ODELL EDUCATION

ORGANIZING EVIDENCE-BASED CLAIMS TOOL (3 POINTS)

Name _ _ _ _ _ _ _ _ _ _ _ _ _ _ _ _ _   Text _

CLAIM:

Point 1

Point 2

Point 3

A	Supporting Evidence

B	Supporting Evidence

C	Supporting Evidence

(Reference:)

(Reference:)

(Reference:)

A	Supporting Evidence

B	Supporting Evidence

C	Supporting Evidence

(Reference:)

(Reference:)

(Reference:)

A	Supporting Evidence

B	Supporting Evidence

C	Supporting Evidence

(Reference:)

(Reference:)

(Reference:)

DELINEATING ARGUMENTS TOOL

Name _____   Topic _____

ISSUE	
PERSPECTIVE	
POSITION	

PREMISE/CLAIM 1	PREMISE/CLAIM 2	PREMISE/CLAIM 3
Supporting evidence:	Supporting evidence:	Supporting evidence:

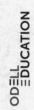
ODELL EDUCATION

BUILDING EVIDENCE-BASED ARGUMENTS LITERACY SKILLS AND ACADEMIC HABITS CHECKLIST

	EVIDENCE-BASED ARGUMENTATION LITERACY SKILLS & ACADEMIC HABITS	✔	EVIDENCE of the SKILLS/HABITS
READING	1. **Recognizing Perspective:** Identifies and explains the author's view of the text's topic.		
	2. **Evaluating Information:** Assesses the relevance and credibility of information in texts.		
	3. **Delineating Argumentation:** Identifies and analyzes the claims, evidence, and reasoning in arguments.		
ACADEMIC HABITS	4. **Remaining Open:** Asks questions of others rather than arguing for a personal idea or opinion.		
	5. **Qualifying Views:** Explains and changes ideas in response to thinking from others.		
	6. **Revising:** Rethinks ideas and refines work based on feedback from others.		
	7. **Reflecting Critically:** Uses literacy concepts to discuss and evaluate personal and peer learning.		
WRITING SKILLS	8. **Forming Claims:** States a meaningful position that is well-supported by evidence from texts.		
	9. **Using Evidence:** Uses well-chosen details from texts to explain and support claims. Accurately paraphrases or quotes.		
	10. **Using Logic:** Supports a position through a logical sequence of related claims, premises, and supporting evidence.		
	11. **Organizing Ideas:** Organizes claims, supporting ideas, and evidence in a logical order.		
	12. **Using Language:** Writes clearly so others can understand claims and ideas.		
	13. **Using Conventions:** Correctly uses sentence elements, punctuation, and spelling to produce clear writing.		
	14. **Publishing:** Correctly uses, formats, and cites textual evidence to support claims.		
	General comments:		

DELINEATING ARGUMENTS: CASE STUDY

Baseball Sharks

ISSUE

It is winter and the parents of an eighth-grader named Jesse are trying to help him determine which baseball team he should play for in the upcoming spring and summer. Jesse is already a fantastic shortstop and pitcher who is being told by his coach that he is better than most high school players. He wants to play with a good team that challenges him but he hates all the travel required by the teams that are really good. Matt is the coach of the best team in the region, the Sharks. The Sharks will travel every weekend from April–July to play in tournaments. Most of these trips are two to three hours or more away. These tournaments are played at colleges and universities and give college coaches and even Major League scouts the opportunity to watch these young athletes compete.

Many of these players are then recruited throughout high school by Major League teams and colleges. Jesse's parents are trying to help him make the best decision and will support him whatever he decides.

Matt, the Shark's coach, is coming over to speak with Jesse and his parents about playing with the Sharks. Jesse's parents are supportive of him and want him to make the best decision for himself.

PERSPECTIVES

COACH MATT

Matt is the Sharks' coach and really wants Jesse to play for him this summer. Matt sees Jesse as a vital piece to his team's success. There are other shortstops that could play for him but none come close to having the skill set Jesse owns. Matt also believes Jesse can play baseball collegiately, and if he continues to get the right type of exposure, he could be drafted into the Major Leagues during high school.

He presents the following argument:

Playing for the Sharks will give you the exposure you need to get an athletic scholarship for college and could lead to you being drafted into Major League Baseball.

Between April and July Jesse will be seen and evaluated by college coaches and Major League scouts. Each tournament provides college coaches and professional scouts access to the best players in the country and enable them to evaluate many players at one time. This access to the decision makers at the next level of competition should be highly valued to someone like Jesse.

The travel schedule is time intensive but a modest price to pay for the opportunities playing collegiate baseball and perhaps professional baseball could provide. We travel a lot. This is because we want our players to have the best possible opportunity to be seen by a variety of coaches from different colleges and universities and be seen by as many professional scouts as possible. It's a sacrifice of time now, but a college scholarship or Major League signing bonus provides a lot of opportunity.

The competition you will face on a nightly basis while playing for the Sharks is incomparable and will make you a better player. Our schedule is demanding and is created to compete against the best teams in the region and the country.

In conclusion, if Jesse wants to play college baseball and be considered professionally, his best chance is to play with the Sharks.

JESSE'S PARENTS

Jesse's parents want to help him make the best decision. They recognize the dilemma he faces and understand the pros and cons of both sides. They feel that Matt is pressuring Jesse to join the Sharks and know the opportunities that playing with them could open up, but they do not want Jesse to make a decision out of pressure or fear.

ODELL
EDUCATION

Baseball Sharks (Continued)

Jesse's parents present the following argument:

Although the Sharks definitely would provide Jesse the best opportunity to pursue a future baseball career, he may not be ready to make this decision. Jesse is an eighth-grader and has several more years before he must decide where he wants to attend school.

Jesse is not ready to commit his entire summer to one activity. Although baseball is important to Jesse, we recognize that being well rounded requires participating in multiple activities and we believe he should get to pursue those that he wants to. Playing on the Sharks would mean he'd have less time at the beach where he loves to swim.

The local team will enable Jesse to continue playing baseball, work on his skills, and not spend all his time on the road. We know the quality and access the local team can provide Jesse are not as good as the Sharks. They're not bad though.

He has been able to develop to this point. And his friend Luke is on the team as well. Playing for the hometown team means he gets to continue playing baseball as well as spend time with his friends.

In conclusion, we want Jesse to have all the information necessary to make the best decision for himself. Although he does want to play baseball collegiately and have the chance to be drafted into Major League Baseball, he is not ready to commit himself completely to just baseball. We want to help Jesse think through both sides of the decision and then support whatever he decides.

OTHER PERSPECTIVES

Jesse, Jesse's older brother, Luke, Jesse's friend

MODEL ARGUMENT: "BASEBALL SHARKS"

Name Model   **Topic** Baseball Sharks—Coach Matt

ISSUE	Eighth-grader Jesse is an excellent baseball player with potential to play in college and the pros. The coach of a highly competitive team wants him to play this summer. Playing on the team would be an incredible opportunity to develop his skills and to play in front of college and pro scouts. The travel required by the team, however, would mean that playing baseball would be just about all he did this summer. He can always play for a less competitive local team that would allow him more time for other activities.
PERSPECTIVE	Matt is the coach of the Sharks. He sees Jesse as a potential key player on his team. He also sees that playing for the Sharks would be good for Jesse's skills and exposure.
POSITION	Jesse should play on the Sharks this summer.

PREMISE/CLAIM 1	PREMISE/CLAIM 2	PREMISE/CLAIM 3
Playing for the Sharks will give Jesse the exposure he needs to get an athletic scholarship for college and could lead to being drafted into Major League Baseball.	The travel schedule is time intensive but a modest price to pay for the opportunities playing collegiate baseball and perhaps professional baseball could provide.	The competition you will face on a nightly basis while playing for the Sharks is incomparable and will make you a better player.
Supporting Evidence	**Supporting Evidence**	**Supporting Evidence**
College and Major League scouts attend the tournaments that the Sharks play.	The intensive travel is because the coach wants the players to play with the best teams around the area at their level. It's a sacrifice of time now, but a college scholarship or Major League signing bonus provides a lot of opportunity.	Our schedule is demanding and is created to compete against the best teams in the region and the country.

MODEL ARGUMENT: "BASEBALL SHARKS"

Name Model

Topic Baseball Sharks—Jesse's Parents

ISSUE	Eighth-grader Jesse is an excellent baseball player with potential to play in college and the pros. The coach of a highly competitive team wants him to play this summer. Playing on the team would be an incredible opportunity to develop his skills and to play in front of college and pro scouts. The travel required by the team, however, would mean that playing baseball would be just about all he did this summer. He can instead play for a less competitive local team that would allow him more time for other activities.
PERSPECTIVE	Jesse's parents support him in everything he does. They recognize he has a gift for baseball and that playing it is and will be important in his life. They also want him to experience many things including just plain enjoying himself. They feel that Jesse is feeling some pressure—especially because the coach is so interested in him. They want him to make the decision without feeling any pressure.
POSITION	Jesse should not play on the Sharks this summer.

PREMISE/CLAIM 1	PREMISE/CLAIM 2	PREMISE/CLAIM 3
Jesse is too young to commit so much time to one activity.	Although the Sharks are better, the hometown team will still give him opportunity to play baseball.	Not playing with the Sharks will give him more time with his friends.
Supporting Evidence	**Supporting Evidence**	**Supporting Evidence**
He has other interests that would suffer from spending so much time playing baseball. He would spend less time swimming at the beach.	He's not giving up playing baseball. So far his experience with the hometown team has been good.	He'll spend less time on the road. And his friend Luke plays on the hometown team, too.

ODELL EDUCATION

DELINEATING ARGUMENTS: CASE STUDY

Friending a Teacher

Mr. Higgins is a twenty-three-year-old social studies teacher at Thunder Ridge Middle School. Over the weekend, he received a friend request on Facebook from Derek, who is one of his students. Derek is a B student who is generally quiet in class. Mr. Higgins has never had a problem with Derek, but he also hasn't interacted with Derek much, either inside or out of class. In order to keep his school life separate from his personal life, Mr. Higgins decided when he took the job at Thunder Ridge that he would not accept a friend request from any of his students. When Derek's parents hear that Mr. Higgins did not accept Derek's request, they scheduled a meeting with Mr. Higgins to demand that he accept the request. They are worried that Mr. Higgins will damage Derek's confidence in school if he continues to reject their son's request.

DEREK

Derek considers himself a technically savvy student. He thinks that social media are fascinating and he is an avid user of Facebook. One of the reasons he likes Facebook is that it gives teachers and students a way to get to know one another outside of class. Derek sent the request to Mr. Higgins in order to include Facebook as part of the learning environment at Thunder Ridge.

At the meeting, Derek explains why he thinks Mr. Higgins should accept his request:

Look, Mr. Higgins. Everyone is on Facebook these days. You should know this because you have a profile and even with your privacy settings I can tell you use it a lot. If you are using Facebook, you should be a good Facebook citizen and accept requests from people. It's just part of the deal. And it's not a big deal. There's no harm in being friends with students. If you post something, you're okay sharing it, so why not let me learn a bit more about you? I mean, I'll find out anyway when I Google you, so it's not like there are a lot of secrets to find. What really makes me mad about rejecting my friend request is that you aren't treating me fairly. I never do anything wrong in class, so there is no reason to reject my request.

MR. HIGGINS

Mr. Higgins is a popular teacher at Thunder Ridge. He is well known for creating new ways to bring technology to the classroom. Most of the students at Thunder Ridge follow him on Twitter. He doesn't hold Derek's request against him, but Mr. Higgins decided before he started his job that accepting friend requests from any student wouldn't be a good idea.

Mr. Higgins explains his decision to Derek:

Even though online platforms are changing the way students and teachers interact, there need to be boundaries. Facebook is a personal space and if I accept your request, I am worried that you'll forget that I am your teacher. There is a further problem to keep in mind. If I accept your request, I am obligated to accept a request from any student. Even if I had a guarantee that you would handle being friends on Facebook appropriately, I cannot be sure about this with everyone, so I don't want to be in a position in which others can accuse me of playing favorites based on what friend requests I accept. And I'd like to ask you, Derek, if you are friends with your parents on Facebook? I'm guessing that you are probably like most of your classmates who don't want to be friends with their parents because they want to keep their social lives private. My Facebook account is no different. It is a place for me to have a life that is separate from my job as your teacher.

OTHER PERSPECTIVES:

Derek's parents, Derek's classmates, Mr. Higgins's colleagues

ODELL
EDUCATION

DELINEATING ARGUMENTS: CASE STUDY

Tweeting about a Pop Quiz

Justin has Spanish class during first period. When the bell rings Monday morning, the teacher announces that there will be a pop quiz. Justin studied over the weekend, so he's confident he did well on the quiz. His friend Mark, however, told Justin on the ride to school that he didn't study at all. Mark has Spanish with the same teacher during third period. Justin decides to Tweet a warning to Mark about the pop quiz so that Mark will have second period to study. Mark sees the Tweet and he studies during his history class.

His grade on the pop quiz is much higher than his average grade for the course, so the teacher becomes suspicious. The teacher eventually finds out that Justin Tweeted a warning to Mark about the quiz. The teacher calls a meeting with Justin and the school principal to inform Justin that the Tweet was cheating and he will be penalized as such. Justin argues that the Tweet isn't cheating and he shouldn't be punished for letting Mark know about the quiz.

THE TEACHER

The teacher has been at the school for more than twenty years. During that time, she has earned a reputation as a hard but fair grader. She has been nominated for teacher of the year several times. She has a policy in her class that cell phones are not allowed to be on.

The teacher explains why she considers the Tweet to be cheating:

When I decide to give a pop quiz, I want to evaluate whether my students are keeping up with the ideas and homework in my course. These quizzes need to be surprises in order to evaluate students' commitment to my course. I don't announce these quizzes ahead of time because this will just encourage students to study at the last minute. This doesn't provide the insight I want into students' performance. Because Justin sent that message to his friend, there was an opportunity for his friend and anyone else who heard about this message to prepare for the quiz. This is an unfair advantage and the grades for the third-period quizzes will almost certainly be higher. This isn't fair to my first-period students. In addition to undermining my quiz, Justin has also created extra work for me. I'll have to redo the quiz at another surprise point in the course. I am going to have to deal with complaints from students who did well on the quiz but will have to take a replacement.

JUSTIN

Justin is a good student. His GPA is a 3.7 and he takes a couple of AP courses. He is also involved in the speech and debate team and the chess club. He glazes hams for extra money on the weekend. He and Mark have been friends for five years, though they aren't best friends. Mark moved to Justin's street so they often see one another over the weekend. Justin knows that Mark struggles with school.

Justin defends his decision to Tweet with the following statement:

Sending a Tweet isn't cheating because I didn't tell Mark or anyone else who saw the Tweet what was on the quiz. I just said that we had a quiz so they might have a quiz. I had no idea if the teacher was going to have a quiz for the third-period class. I can't read her mind. What I did isn't different from the other students who told their friends about the quiz in person. Besides, couldn't Mark have thought there might be a quiz even if he hadn't seen the Tweet? At the end of the day, Mark studied and did well, so I don't see what the problem is. It doesn't matter what I Tweeted or what he thought. What matters is that he spent time preparing for the quiz and he earned his grade.

OTHER PERSPECTIVES

Other students, the principal, the teacher's colleagues

NOTES